# GREAT JOBS

## FOR

# Accounting Majors

Jan Goldberg

## McGraw·Hill

New York   Chicago   San Francisco   Lisbon   London   Madrid   Mexico City
Milan   New Delhi   San Juan   Seoul   Singapore   Sydney   Toronto

The *McGraw·Hill* Companies

**Library of Congress Cataloging-in-Publication Data**

Goldberg, Jan.
      Great jobs for accounting majors / Jan Goldberg. — 2nd ed.
         p.    cm.
      Includes index.
      ISBN 0-07-143854-8 (alk. paper)
      1. Accounting—Vocational guidance—United States.    I. Title.

  HF5616.U5G643    2005
  657'.023'73—dc22                      2004059737

1 2 3 4 5 6 7 8 9 0  DOC/DOC  0 9 8 7 6 5

ISBN 0-07-143854-8

McGraw-Hill books are available at special quantity discounts to use as premiums and sales promotions, or for use in corporate training programs. For more information, please write to the Director of Special Sales, Professional Publishing, McGraw-Hill, Two Penn Plaza, New York, NY 10121-2298. Or contact your local bookstore.

This book is printed on acid-free paper.

To the memory of my father and mother,
Sam and Sylvia Lefkovitz,
and a special aunt, Estelle Lefko,
for always encouraging me to follow my dreams.

# Contents

# Acknowledgments

The author gratefully acknowledges the professionals who graciously agreed to be profiled within this text, as well as the associations and organizations that provided valuable and interesting information.

Thanks to my dear husband, Larry, daughters, Sherri and Debbie, son-in-law, Bruce, sister, Adrienne, and brother, Paul, for their encouragement and support.

Thanks also to family and close friends: Michele, Alison, Steven, Marty, Mindi, Cary, Michele, Marci, Steven, Brian, Jesse, Bertha, Uncle Bernard, and Aunt Helen.

A special thanks to a special friend, Diana Catlin.

Sincere gratitude to Betsy Lancefield, former editor at McGraw-Hill, for providing this challenging opportunity and her help whenever and wherever it is needed.

The editors would like to thank Deb Garvey for preparing this second edition.

# Introduction

## *Accounting: A Degree That Adds Up*

*"Of all debts—men are least willing to pay the taxes. What a satire is this on government! Everywhere they think they get their money's worth, except for these."*
—RALPH WALDO EMERSON

Evidence exists that shows accounting practices were already in use more than five thousand years ago. Some of the earliest accounting records were written on papyrus and clay tablets in cuneiform and hieroglyphics. Besides ancient picture writing, cuneiform is considered to be the oldest kind of writing in the world, a system invented by the ancient Sumerians around 3000 B.C.

Even the Bible makes mention of accounting, noting that proper accounting between people can lessen arguments and disagreements. Other evidence of accounting practices from approximately 600 B.C. has been credited to ancient Roman businesses and household records. Accounting in China and Asia dates back to the very distant past.

Modern accounting dates from fifteenth-century Italy, when, during the height of trading, bookkeeping was required to keep track of the import and export of goods. As new accounting procedures were created and practiced widely, the need for trained professionals soon became apparent.

The first known college of accounting was a guild established in Venice, Italy, in the sixteenth century. Training consisted of a six-year apprenticeship program followed by an examination.

From Italy, which remained a leader in accounting until the eighteenth century, the practice of accounting spread throughout Europe to England, and from there to the New World. An accounting society was established in Edinburgh, Scotland, in 1854, coinciding with the beginning of the Industrial Revolution. The Industrial Revolution created a need for systematic bookkeeping, which became the primary responsibility of managerial assistants. Sometimes experts were hired to teach the owner of a small business how to keep the books or to verify figures or discover errors in financial records.

In 1887, the American Association of Public Accountants became the first organization of public accountants. Today it is known as the American Institute of Certified Public Accountants. Ten years after the founding of the association, the state of New York enacted laws setting minimum standards for those engaging in public accounting and adopted a procedure for licensing. In time, all states passed similar legislation.

Passage of the Sixteenth Amendment to the U.S. Constitution in 1913 provided for taxation of income. Accountants began to prepare income tax returns, becoming authorities on ever-changing regulations and advising individuals and businesses on tax matters. Eventually tax preparers began to advise individuals and businesses on financial planning for the future, one of the most important responsibilities tax professionals hold to this day.

## The Importance of Education

While it is true that having a college degree will not guarantee you a position in the world of accounting, it is important to realize that this is the best way to prepare yourself for and increase your opportunities in the job market. Most employers will not even consider you for a position if you are lacking a four-year degree in accounting or a related field. No matter what career you choose, a higher education will

- Offer a broad base of knowledge and experiences
- Allow you to increase and perfect your skills
- Provide you with opportunities to gain important personal and professional contacts
- Give you the information you need to make an informed career decision

To succeed in today's highly competitive job market, you have to be one of the cream of the crop. This requires a plan of action: What degree will you pursue? Which college will you attend? What is the ideal internship? How much graduate course work will you complete? What area of specialization is of interest to you? What are the licensure and professional certification requirements for your career choice? Once you have a plan, you need to follow it, modifying it along the way to best suit your career goal. With book knowledge, work experience, flexibility, and a positive attitude, success should be yours.

# PART ONE

# THE JOB SEARCH

# 1

# The Self-Assessment

Self-assessment is the process by which you begin to acknowledge your own particular blend of education, experiences, values, needs, and goals. It provides the foundation for career planning and the entire job search process. Self-assessment involves looking inward and asking yourself what can sometimes prove to be difficult questions. This self-examination should lead to an intimate understanding of your personal traits, your personal values, your consumption patterns and economic needs, your longer-term goals, your skill base, your preferred skills, and your underdeveloped skills.

You come to the self-assessment process knowing yourself well in some of these areas, but you may still be uncertain about other aspects. You may be well aware of your consumption patterns, but have you spent much time specifically identifying your longer-term goals or your personal values as they relate to work? No matter what level of self-assessment you have undertaken to date, it is now time to clarify all of these issues and questions as they relate to the job search.

The knowledge you gain in the self-assessment process will guide the rest of your job search. In this book, you will learn about all of the following tasks:

- Writing résumés and cover letters
- Researching careers and networking
- Interviewing and job offer considerations

In each of these steps, you will rely on and often return to the understanding gained through your self-assessment. Any individual seeking employment must be able and willing to express these facets of his or her personality

3

to recruiters and interviewers throughout the job search. This communication allows you to show the world who you are so that together with employers you can determine whether there will be a workable match with a given job or career path.

## How to Conduct a Self-Assessment

The self-assessment process goes on naturally all the time. People ask you to clarify what you mean, you make a purchasing decision, or you begin a new relationship. You react to the world and the world reacts to you. How you understand these interactions and any changes you might make because of them are part of the natural process of self-discovery. There is, however, a more comprehensive and efficient way to approach self-assessment with regard to employment.

Because self-assessment can become a complex exercise, we have distilled it into a seven-step process that provides an effective basis for undertaking a job search. The seven steps include the following:

1. Understanding your personal traits
2. Identifying your personal values
3. Calculating your economic needs
4. Exploring your longer-term goals
5. Enumerating your skill base
6. Recognizing your preferred skills
7. Assessing skills needing further development

As you work through your self-assessment, you might want to create a worksheet similar to the one shown in Exhibit 1.1, starting on the following page. Or you might want to keep a journal of the thoughts you have as you undergo this process. There will be many opportunities to revise your self-assessment as you start down the path of seeking a career.

### Step 1    Understand Your Personal Traits
Each person has a unique personality that he or she brings to the job search process. Gaining a better understanding of your personal traits can help you evaluate job and career choices. Identifying these traits and then finding employment that allows you to draw on at least some of them can create a rewarding and fulfilling work experience. If potential employment doesn't allow you to use these preferred traits, it is important to decide whether you

Exhibit 1.1
## SELF-ASSESSMENT WORKSHEET

**Step 1. Understand Your Personal Traits**
The personal traits that describe me are:
*(Include all of the words that describe you.)*
The ten personal traits that most accurately describe me are:
*(List these ten traits.)*

**Step 2. Identify Your Personal Values**
Working conditions that are important to me include:
*(List working conditions that would have to exist for you to accept a position.)*
The values that go along with my working conditions are:
*(Write down the values that correspond to each working condition.)*
Some additional values I've decided to include are:
*(List those values you identify as you conduct this job search.)*

**Step 3. Calculate Your Economic Needs**
My estimated minimum annual salary requirement is:
*(Write the salary you have calculated based on your budget.)*
Starting salaries for the positions I'm considering are:
*(List the name of each job you are considering and the associated starting salary.)*

**Step 4. Explore Your Longer-Term Goals**
My thoughts on longer-term goals right now are:
*(Jot down some of your longer-term goals as you know them right now.)*

**Step 5. Enumerate Your Skill Base**
The general skills I possess are:
*(List the skills that underlie tasks you are able to complete.)*
The specific skills I possess are:
*(List more technical or specific skills that you possess, and indicate your level of expertise.)*
General and specific skills that I want to promote to employers for the jobs I'm considering are:
*(List general and specific skills for each type of job you are considering.)*

*continued*

---

**Step 6. Recognize Your Preferred Skills**

Skills that I would like to use on the job include:

(List skills that you hope to use on the job, and indicate how often you'd like to use them.)

**Step 7. Assess Skills Needing Further Development**

Some skills that I'll need to acquire for the jobs I'm considering include:

(Write down skills listed in job advertisements or job descriptions that you don't currently possess.)

I believe I can build these skills by:

(Describe how you plan to acquire these skills.)

---

can find other ways to express them or whether you would be better off not considering this type of job. Interests and hobbies pursued outside of work hours can be one way to use personal traits you don't have an opportunity to draw on in your work. For example, if you consider yourself an outgoing person and the kinds of jobs you are examining allow little contact with other people, you may be able to achieve the level of interaction that is comfortable for you outside of your work setting. If such a compromise seems impractical or otherwise unsatisfactory, you probably should explore only jobs that provide the interaction you want and need on the job.

Many young adults who are not very confident about their employability will downplay their need for income. They will say, "Money is not all that important if I love my work." But if you begin to document exactly what you need for housing, transportation, insurance, clothing, food, and utilities, you will begin to understand that some jobs cannot meet your financial needs and it doesn't matter how wonderful the job is. If you have to worry each payday about bills and other financial obligations, you won't be very effective on the job. Begin now to be honest with yourself about your needs.

Begin the self-assessment process by creating an inventory of your personal traits. Make a list of as many words as possible to describe yourself. Words like *accurate, creative, future-oriented, relaxed,* or *structured* are just a few examples. In addition, you might ask people who know you well how they might describe you.

**Focus on Selected Personal Traits.** Of all the traits you identified, select the ten you believe most accurately describe you. Keep track of these ten traits.

**Consider Your Personal Traits in the Job Search Process.** As you begin exploring jobs and careers, watch for matches between your personal traits and the job descriptions you read. Some jobs will require many personal traits you know you possess, and others will not seem to match those traits.

---

For example, a management accountant can work for a large corporation as part of a team that is developing a new product line. Excellent organizational and interpersonal skills are essential qualities for someone who will work with other departments and supervisors. Self-employed public accountants, on the other hand, usually work alone, interacting only with clients. Both often have deadlines to meet, but the public accountant has far fewer people to answer to and must be able to work independently.

---

Your ability to respond to changing conditions, your decision-making ability, productivity, creativity, and verbal skills all have a bearing on your success in and enjoyment of your work life. To better guarantee success, be sure to take the time needed to understand these traits in yourself.

## Step 2   Identify Your Personal Values

Your personal values affect every aspect of your life, including employment, and they develop and change as you move through life. Values can be defined as principles that we hold in high regard, qualities that are important and desirable to us. Some values aren't ordinarily connected to work (love, beauty, color, light, relationships, family, or religion), and others are (autonomy, cooperation, effectiveness, achievement, knowledge, and security). Our values determine, in part, the level of satisfaction we feel in a particular job.

**Define Acceptable Working Conditions.** One facet of employment is the set of working conditions that must exist for someone to consider taking a job.

Each of us would probably create a unique list of acceptable working conditions, but items that might be included on many people's lists are the amount of money you would need to be paid, how far you are willing to drive or travel, the amount of freedom you want in determining your own schedule, whether you would be working with people or data or things, and the types of tasks you would be willing to do. Your conditions might include statements of working conditions you will *not* accept; for example, you might not be willing to work at night or on weekends or holidays.

If you were offered a job tomorrow, what conditions would have to exist for you to realistically consider accepting the position? Take some time and make a list of these conditions.

**Realize Associated Values.** Your list of working conditions can be used to create an inventory of your values relating to jobs and careers you are exploring. For example, if one of your conditions stated that you wanted to earn at least $30,000 per year, the associated value would be financial gain. If another condition was that you wanted to work with a friendly group of people, the value that went along with that might be belonging or interaction with people.

**Relate Your Values to the World of Work.** As you read the job descriptions you come across either in this book, in newspapers and magazines, or online, think about the values associated with each position.

---

For example, the duties of an Internal Revenue Service agent would include researching, investigating, and conducting interviews; working with customers, businesses, and staff at all levels of financial institutions; and working with the latest technology. Some of the associated values are precision, communication, cooperation, and knowledge.

---

At least some of the associated values in the field you're exploring should match those you extracted from your list of working conditions. Take a second look at any values that don't match up. How important are they to you? What will happen if they are not satisfied on the job? Can you incorporate those personal values elsewhere? Your answers need to be brutally honest. As you continue your exploration, be sure to add to your list any additional values that occur to you.

## Step 3  Calculate Your Economic Needs
Each of us grew up in an environment that provided for certain basic needs, such as food and shelter, and, to varying degrees, other needs that we now consider basic, such as cable television, e-mail, or an automobile. Needs such as privacy, space, and quiet, which at first glance may not appear to be monetary needs, may add to housing expenses and so should be considered as you examine your economic needs. For example, if you place a high value

on a large, open living space for yourself, it would be difficult to satisfy that need without an associated high housing cost, especially in a densely populated city environment.

As you prepare to move into the world of work and become responsible for meeting your own basic needs, it is important to consider the salary you will need to be able to afford a satisfying standard of living. The three-step process outlined here will help you plan a budget, which in turn will allow you to evaluate the various career choices and geographic locations you are considering. The steps include (1) developing a realistic budget, (2) examining starting salaries, and (3) using a cost-of-living index.

**Develop a Realistic Budget.** Each of us has certain expectations for the kind of lifestyle we want to maintain. To begin the process of defining your economic needs, it will be helpful to determine what you expect to spend on routine monthly expenses. These expenses include housing, food, transportation, entertainment, utilities, loan repayments, and revolving charge accounts. You may not currently spend anything for certain items, but you probably will have to once you begin supporting yourself. As you develop this budget, be generous in your estimates, but keep in mind any items that could be reduced or eliminated. If you are not sure about the cost of a certain item, talk with family or friends who would be able to give you a realistic estimate.

If this is new or difficult for you, start to keep a log of expenses right now. You may be surprised at how much you actually spend each month for food or stamps or magazines. Household expenses and personal grooming items can often loom very large in a budget, as can auto repairs or home maintenance.

Income taxes must also be taken into consideration when examining salary requirements. State and local taxes vary, so it is difficult to calculate exactly the effect of taxes on the amount of income you need to generate. To roughly estimate the gross income necessary to generate your minimum annual salary requirement, multiply the minimum salary you have calculated by a factor of 1.35. The resulting figure will be an approximation of what your gross income would need to be, given your estimated expenses.

**Examine Starting Salaries.** Starting salaries for each of the career tracks are provided throughout this book. These salary figures can be used in conjunction with the cost-of-living index (discussed in the next section) to determine whether you would be able to meet your basic economic needs in a given geographic location.

**Use a Cost-of-Living Index.** If you are thinking about trying to get a job in a geographic region other than the one where you now live, understanding differences in the cost of living will help you come to a more informed decision about making a move. By using a cost-of-living index, you can compare salaries offered and the cost of living in different locations with what you know about the salaries offered and the cost of living in your present location.

Many variables are used to calculate the cost-of-living index. Often included are housing, groceries, utilities, transportation, health care, clothing, and entertainment expenses. Right now you do not need to worry about the details associated with calculating a given index. The main purpose of this exercise is to help you understand that pay ranges for entry-level positions may not vary greatly, but the cost of living in different locations *can* vary tremendously.

Suppose you live in Cleveland, Ohio, and you are interested in working as a high school accounting teacher in the Cleveland School District. The U.S. Department of Labor's Bureau of Labor Statistics (bls.gov) reports that the average salary for secondary school teachers in Cleveland is $44,170 annually. But let's say you're thinking about moving to either Boston, Los Angeles, or Minneapolis. You know you can live on $44,170 in Cleveland, but you want to be able to equal that salary in other locations you're considering. How much will you need to earn in those locations to do this? Figuring the cost of living for each city will show you.

## JOB: HIGH SCHOOL ACCOUNTING TEACHER

| City | Index | Equivalent Salary |
|------|-------|-------------------|
| Boston | 138.0 | |
| | | $\dfrac{138.0}{105.6} \times \$44,170 = \$57,722$ in Boston |
| Cleveland | 105.6 | |
| Los Angeles | 149.9 | |
| | | $\dfrac{149.9}{105.6} \times \$44,170 = \$62,700$ in Los Angeles |
| Cleveland | 105.6 | |
| Minneapolis | 114.0 | |
| | | $\dfrac{114.0}{105.6} \times \$44,170 = \$47,684$ in Minneapolis |
| Cleveland | 105.6 | |

Let's walk through this example. In any cost-of-living index, the number 100 represents the national average cost of living and each city is assigned an index number based on current prices in that city for the items included in the index (housing, food, etc.). In the index used in this example, Boston was assigned the number 138.0, Los Angeles's index was 149.9, Minneapolis's was 114.0, and Cleveland's index was 105.6. In other words, it costs nearly one and a half times as much to live in Los Angeles as it does in Cleveland. The previous table indicates that you would have to earn $57,722 in Boston, $62,700 in Los Angeles, and $47,684 in Minneapolis to match the buying power of $44,170 in Cleveland.

If you would like to determine whether it's financially worthwhile to make any of these moves, one more piece of information is needed: the salaries of high school accounting teachers in these other cities. The following table compares median salaries for these three locations with salaries equivalent to Cleveland's:

| City | Median Annual Salary | Salary Equivalent to Cleveland's | Change in Buying Power |
|------|----------------------|----------------------------------|------------------------|
| Boston | $48,870 | $57,722 | −$8,852 |
| Los Angeles | $57,150 | $62,700 | −$5,550 |
| Minneapolis | $44,110 | $47,684 | −$3,574 |
| Cleveland | $44,170 | — | — |

If you moved to Boston, Los Angeles, or Minneapolis as a high school accounting teacher, you would not be able to maintain a lifestyle similar to the one you would lead in Cleveland with the same job and years of service. In any of these relocation scenarios, you would decrease your buying power given the rate of pay and cost of living in these cities.

You can work through a similar exercise for any type of job you are considering and for many locations when current salary information is available. It will be worth your time to undertake this analysis if you are seriously considering a relocation. By doing so you will be able to make an informed choice.

## Step 4 Explore Your Longer-Term Goals

There is no question that when we first begin working, our goals are to use our skills and education in a job that will reward us with employment, income, and status relative to the preparation we brought with us to this position. If we are not being paid as much as we feel we should for our level of education or if job demands don't provide the intellectual stimulation we had hoped for, we experience unhappiness and as a result often seek other employment.

Most jobs we consider "good" are those that fulfill our basic "lower-level" needs of security, food, clothing, shelter, income, and productive work. But even when our basic needs are met and our jobs are secure and productive, we as individuals are constantly changing. As we change, the demands and expectations we place on our jobs may change. Fortunately, some jobs grow and change with us, and this explains why some people are happy throughout many years in a job.

But more often people are bigger than the jobs they fill. We have more goals and needs than any job could satisfy. These are "higher-level" needs of self-esteem, companionship, affection, and an increasing desire to feel we are employing ourselves in the most effective way possible. Not all of these higher-level needs can be met through employment, but for as long as we are employed, we increasingly demand that our jobs play their part in moving us along the path to fulfillment.

Another obvious but important fact is that we change as we mature. Although our jobs also have the potential for change, they may not change as frequently or as markedly as we do. There are increasingly fewer one-job, one-employer careers; we must think about a work future that may involve voluntary or forced moves from employer to employer. Because of that very real possibility, we need to take advantage of the opportunities in each position we hold. Acquiring the skills and competencies associated with each position will keep us viable and attractive as employees. This is particularly true in a job market that not only is technology/computer dependent, but also is populated with more and more small, self-transforming organizations rather than the large, seemingly stable organizations of the past.

---

If you are considering a position as an IRS agent, you will gain a better perspective on this career by talking to employees in different divisions (e.g., the Small Business and Self-Employed Division or the Tax-Exempt and Government Entities Division) who hold different levels of responsibility: an entry-level field employee, a more experienced revenue agent, and, finally, a member of management who has a considerable work history with the IRS. Each will have a different perspective, unique concerns, and an individual set of priorities.

---

## Step 5   Enumerate Your Skill Base

In terms of the job search, skills can be thought of as capabilities that can be developed in school, at work, or by volunteering and then used in specific job settings. Many studies have documented the kinds of skills that employers seek in entry-level applicants. For example, some of the most desired skills for individuals interested in the teaching profession are the ability to interact effectively with students one-on-one, to manage a classroom, to adapt to varying situations as necessary, and to get involved in school activities. Business employers have also identified important qualities, including enthusiasm for the employer's product or service, a businesslike mind, the ability to follow written or oral instructions, the ability to demonstrate self-control, the confidence to suggest new ideas, the ability to communicate with all members of a group, an awareness of cultural differences, and loyalty, to name just a few. You will find that many of these skills are also in the repertoire of qualities demanded in your college major.

To be successful in obtaining any given job, you must be able to demonstrate that you possess a certain mix of skills that will allow you to carry out the duties required by that job. This skill mix will vary a great deal from job to job; to determine the skills necessary for the jobs you are seeking, you can read job advertisements or more generic job descriptions, such as those found later in this book. If you want to be effective in the job search, you must directly show employers that you possess the skills needed to be successful in filling the position. These skills will initially be described on your résumé and then discussed again during the interview process.

Skills are either general or specific. To develop a list of skills relevant to employers, you must first identify the general skills you possess, then list specific skills you have to offer, and, finally, examine which of these skills employers are seeking.

*Identify Your General Skills.*  Because you possess or will possess a college degree, employers will assume that you can read and write, perform certain basic computations, think critically, and communicate effectively. Employers will want to see that you have acquired these skills, and they will want to know which additional general skills you possess.

One way to begin identifying skills is to write an experiential diary. An experiential diary lists all the tasks you were responsible for completing for each job you've held and then outlines the skills required to do those tasks. You may list several skills for any given task. This diary allows you to distinguish between the tasks you performed and the underlying skills required to complete those tasks. Here's an example:

| Tasks | Skills |
|---|---|
| Answering telephone | Effective use of language, clear diction, ability to direct inquiries, ability to solve problems |
| Waiting on tables | Poise under conditions of time and pressure, speed, accuracy, good memory, simultaneous completion of tasks, sales skills |

For each job or experience you have participated in, develop a worksheet based on the example shown here. On a résumé, you may want to describe these skills rather than simply listing tasks. Skills are easier for the employer to appreciate, especially when your experience is very different from the employment you are seeking. In addition to helping you identify general skills, this experiential diary will prepare you to speak more effectively in an interview about the qualifications you possess.

**Identify Your Specific Skills.** It may be easier to identify your specific skills because you can definitely say whether you can speak other languages, program a computer, draft a map or diagram, or edit a document using appropriate symbols and terminology.

Using your experiential diary, identify the points in your history where you learned how to do something very specific, and decide whether you have a beginning, intermediate, or advanced knowledge of how to use that particular skill. Right now, be sure to list *every* specific skill you have, and don't consider whether you like using the skill. Write down a list of specific skills you have acquired and the level of competence you possess—beginning, intermediate, or advanced.

**Relate Your Skills to Employers.** You probably have thought about a couple of different jobs you might be interested in obtaining, and one way to begin relating the general and specific skills you possess to a potential employer's needs is to read actual advertisements for these types of positions (see Part Two for resources listing actual job openings).

For example, you might be interested in a career as an auditor with a CPA firm. A typical job listing might read, "Requires 2 to 5 years' experience, organizational and interpersonal skills, analytical ability, drive, and the ability to work under pressure." You could find more information in a general source that describes the job of an auditor, where you would learn that auditors also design internal control systems, analyze financial data, work with statistics, and must be thoroughly knowledgeable about computer information systems.

Begin building a comprehensive list of required skills with the first job description you read. Exploring advertisements for and descriptions of several types of related positions will reveal an important core of skills necessary for obtaining the type of work you're interested in. In building the list, include both general and specific skills.

Following is a sample list of skills needed to be successful as an auditor. These items were extracted from general resources and actual job listings.

## JOB: AUDITOR

| General Skills | Specific Skills |
| --- | --- |
| Ability to gather and interpret information | Write reports |
| | Prepare financial reports |
| Possession of a specific body of knowledge | Verify records |
| | Inspect accounting systems |
| Familiarity with computer systems | Master various software |
| Ability to work independently | Deliver oral reports |
| Ability to work well with other people | Design control systems |
| Strong written and verbal skills | Calculate taxes |
| Organizational skills | Investigate mismanagement |
| Integrity | Advise clients |

On a separate sheet of paper, try to generate a comprehensive list of required skills for at least one job you are considering. The list of general skills that you develop for a given career path will be valuable for any number of jobs you might apply for. Many of the specific skills will also be transferable to other positions. For example, the ability to understand a business system to investigate the possibility of mismanagement would be a required skill not only for auditors but also for management consultants.

## Step 6　Recognize Your Preferred Skills

In the previous section you developed a comprehensive list of skills that relate to particular career paths that are of interest to you. You can now relate these to skills that you prefer to use. We all use a wide range of skills (some researchers say individuals have a repertoire of about five hundred skills), but we may not particularly be interested in using all of them in our work. There may be some skills that come to us more naturally or that we use successfully time and time again and that we want to continue to use; these are best described as our preferred skills. For this exercise use the list of skills that you created for the previous section, and decide which of them you are *most interested in using* in future work and how often you would like to use them. You might be interested in using some skills only occasionally, while others you would like to use more regularly. You probably also have skills that you hope you can use constantly.

As you examine job announcements, look for matches between this list of preferred skills and the qualifications described in the advertisements. These skills should be highlighted on your résumé and discussed in job interviews.

## Step 7　Assess Skills Needing Further Development

Previously you compiled a list of general and specific skills required for given positions. You already possess some of these skills; those that remain to be developed are your underdeveloped skills.

If you are just beginning the job search, there may be gaps between the qualifications required for some of the jobs you're considering and the skills you possess. The thought of having to admit to and talk about these underdeveloped skills, especially in a job interview, is a frightening one. One way to put a healthy perspective on this subject is to target and relate your exploration of underdeveloped skills to the types of positions you are seeking. Recognizing these shortcomings and planning to overcome them with either on-the-job training or additional formal education can be a positive way to address the concept of underdeveloped skills.

On your worksheet or in your journal, make a list of up to five general or specific skills required for the positions you're interested in that you *don't currently possess*. For each item list an idea you have for specific action you could take to acquire that skill. Do some brainstorming to come up with possible actions. If you have a hard time generating ideas, talk to people currently working in this type of position, professionals in your college career services office, trusted friends, family members, or members of related professional associations.

In the chapter on interviewing, we will discuss in detail how to effectively address questions about underdeveloped skills. Generally speaking, though, employers want genuine answers to these types of questions. They want you to reveal "the real you," and they also want to see how you answer difficult questions. In taking the positive, targeted approach discussed previously, you show the employer that you are willing to continue to learn and that you have a plan for strengthening your job qualifications.

## Use Your Self-Assessment

Exploring entry-level career options can be an exciting experience if you have good resources available and will take the time to use them. Can you effectively complete the following tasks?

1. Understand your personality traits and relate them to career choices
2. Define your personal values
3. Determine your economic needs
4. Explore longer-term goals
5. Understand your skill base
6. Recognize your preferred skills
7. Express a willingness to improve on your underdeveloped skills

If so, then you can more meaningfully participate in the job search process by writing a more effective résumé, finding job titles that represent work you are interested in doing, locating job sites that will provide the opportunity for you to use your strengths and skills, networking in an informed way, participating in focused interviews, getting the most out of follow-up contacts, and evaluating job offers to find those that create a good match between you and the employer. The remaining chapters in Part One guide you through these next steps in the job search process. For many job seekers, this process can take anywhere from three months to a year to implement. The time you will need to put into your job search will depend on the type of job you want and the geographic location where you'd like to work. Think of your effort as a job in itself, requiring you to set aside time each week to complete the needed work. Carefully undertaken efforts may reduce the time you need for your job search.

# 2

# The Résumé and Cover Letter

The task of writing a résumé may seem overwhelming if you are unfamiliar with this type of document, but there are some easily understood techniques that can and should be used. This section was written to help you understand the purpose of the résumé, the different types of résumé formats available, and how to write the sections of information traditionally found on a résumé. We will present examples and explanations that address questions frequently posed by people writing their first résumé or updating an old résumé.

Even within the formats and suggestions given, however, there are infinite variations. True, most résumés follow one of the outlines suggested, but you should feel free to adjust the résumé to suit your needs and make it expressive of your life and experience.

## Why Write a Résumé?

The purpose of a résumé is to convince an employer that you should be interviewed. Whether you're mailing, faxing, or e-mailing this document, you'll want to present enough information to show that you can make an immediate and valuable contribution to an organization. A résumé is not an indepth historical or legal document; later in the job search process you may be asked to document your entire work history on an application form and attest to its validity. The résumé should, instead, highlight relevant information pertaining directly to the organization that will receive the document or to the type of position you are seeking.

We will discuss the chronological and digital résumés in detail here. Functional and targeted résumés, which are used much less often, are briefly discussed. The reasons for using one type of résumé over another and the typical format for each are addressed in the following sections.

## The Chronological Résumé

The chronological résumé is the most common of the various résumé formats and therefore the format that employers are most used to receiving. This type of résumé is easy to read and understand because it details the chronological progression of jobs you have held. (See Exhibit 2.1.) It begins with your most recent employment and works back in time. If you have a solid work history or have experience that provided growth and development in your duties and responsibilities, a chronological résumé will highlight these achievements. The typical elements of a chronological résumé include the heading, a career objective, educational background, employment experience, activities, and references.

### The Heading
The heading consists of your name, address, telephone number, and other means of contact. This may include a fax number, e-mail address, and your home-page address. If you are using a shared e-mail account or a parent's business fax, be sure to let others who use these systems know that you may receive important professional correspondence via these systems. You wouldn't want to miss a vital e-mail or fax! Likewise, if your résumé directs readers to a personal home page on the Web, be certain it's a professional personal home page designed to be viewed and appreciated by a prospective employer. This may mean making substantial changes in the home page you currently mount on the Web.

### The Objective
Without a doubt the objective statement is the most challenging part of the résumé for most writers. Even for individuals who have decided on a career path, it can be difficult to encapsulate all they want to say in one or two brief sentences. For job seekers who are unfocused or unclear about their intentions, trying to write this section can inhibit the entire résumé writing process.

Keep the objective as short as possible and no longer than two short sentences.

Exhibit 2.1
## CHRONOLOGICAL RÉSUMÉ

### ANN PARKER
3400 El Camino Real
Boca Raton, FL 33432
(561) 555-7890
aparker@site.com

**OBJECTIVE**

A career as a management accountant for a large corporation or health-care facility, ultimately working with internal auditing

**EDUCATION**

Bachelor of Arts in Accounting
Florida Atlantic University
Boca Raton, Florida
May 2004
Overall GPA 3.2 on a 4.0 scale

**RELATED COURSES**

Information Systems Design    Internal Auditing
Workplace Communications    Professional Writing

**EXPERIENCE**

Internship
Motorola Corporation
Fort Lauderdale, Florida
2003 to Present
Assistant to the Associate Financial Director
Examined financial records, wrote reports

Summer Work-Study Program
Boca Raton Community Hospital
Summers 2001 to 2003
Bookkeeping Department
Assisted with payroll and withholding tax deductions

*continued*

**PORTFOLIO**

Portfolio of projects completed during the internship is available upon request.

**COMMUNITY SERVICE**

Volunteer, Medical Records Department, North Broward General Hospital; Intake Processor, Student Red Cross Blood Drive (two years), Florida Atlantic University

**REFERENCES**

Personal and professional references are available upon request.

Choose one of the following types of objective statement:

## 1. *General Objective Statement*

- An entry-level educational programming coordinator position

## 2. *Position-Focused Objective*

- To obtain the position of conference coordinator at State College

## 3. *Industry-Focused Objective*

- To begin a career as a sales representative in the cruise line industry

## 4. *Summary of Qualifications Statement*

A degree in accounting and three years of progressively increasing responsibility in the financial department of a local corporation have prepared me for a career as a management accountant in an institution that values teamwork, integrity, and attention to detail.

***Support Your Objective.*** A résumé that contains any one of these types of objective statements should then go on to demonstrate why you are qualified to get the position. Listing academic degrees can be one way to indicate qualifications. Another demonstration would be in the way previous experiences, both volunteer and paid, are described. Without this kind of documentation in the body of the résumé, the objective looks unsupported. Think of the résumé as telling a connected story about you. All the elements should work together to form a coherent picture that ideally should relate to your statement of objective.

## Education

This section of your résumé should indicate the exact name of the degree you will receive or have received, spelled out completely with no abbreviations. The degree is generally listed after the objective, followed by the institution name and location, and then the month and year of graduation. This section could also include your academic minor, grade point average (GPA), and appearance on the Dean's List or President's List.

If you have enough space, you might want to include a section listing courses related to the field in which you are seeking work. The best use of a "related courses" section would be to list some course work that is not traditionally associated with the major. Perhaps you took several computer courses outside your degree that will be helpful and related to the job prospects you are entertaining. Several education section examples are shown here:

---

- Bachelor of Science Degree in Accounting; University of Maryland University College; Adelphi, Maryland; May 2005; Minor: Human Resource Management
- Bachelor of Arts Degree in Accounting; Taylor University; Upland, Indiana; May 2005; Minor: Computer Science
- Bachelor of Science Degree in Accounting; St. Mary's College of California; Moraga, California; June 2005; Minor: Economics

An example of a format for a related courses section follows:

RELATED COURSES

| | |
|---|---|
| Corporate Finance | Computer Applications |
| Economics | Business Research Design |
| Real Estate Investment | |

---

## Experience

The experience section of your résumé should be the most substantial part and should take up most of the space on the page. Employers want to see what kind of work history you have. They will look at your range of experiences, longevity in jobs, and specific tasks you are able to complete. This section may also be called "work experience," "related experience," "employment history," or "employment." No matter what you call this section, some important points to remember are the following:

1. **Describe your duties** as they relate to the position you are seeking.
2. **Emphasize major responsibilities** and indicate increases in responsibility. Include all relevant employment experiences: summer, part-time, internships, cooperative education, or self-employment.
3. **Emphasize skills**, especially those that transfer from one situation to another. The fact that you coordinated a student organization, chaired meetings, supervised others, and managed a budget leads one to suspect that you could coordinate other things as well.
4. **Use descriptive job titles** that provide information about what you did. A "Student Intern" should be more specifically stated as, for example, "Magazine Operations Intern." "Volunteer" is also too general; a title such as "Peer Writing Tutor" would be more appropriate.
5. **Create word pictures** by using active verbs to start sentences. Describe *results* you have produced in the work you have done.

A limp description would say something such as the following: "My duties included helping with production, proofreading, and editing. I used a design and page layout program." An action statement would be stated as follows: "Coordinated and assisted in the creative marketing of brochures and seminar promotions, becoming proficient in Quark."

Remember, an accomplishment is simply a result, a final measurable product that people can relate to. A duty is not a result; it is an obligation—every job holder has duties. For an effective résumé, list as many results as you can. To make the most of the limited space you have and to give your description impact, carefully select appropriate and accurate descriptors.

Here are some traits that employers tell us they like to see:

- Teamwork
- Energy and motivation

- Learning and using new skills
- Versatility
- Critical thinking
- Understanding how profits are created
- Organizational acumen
- Communicating directly and clearly, in both writing and speaking
- Risk taking
- Willingness to admit mistakes
- High personal standards

## Solutions to Frequently Encountered Problems

### Repetitive Employment with the Same Employer
EMPLOYMENT: The Foot Locker, Portland, Oregon. Summer 2001, 2002, 2003. Initially employed in high school as salesclerk. Due to successful performance, asked to return next two summers at higher pay with added responsibility. Ranked as the #2 salesperson the first summer and #1 the next two summers. Assisted in arranging eye-catching retail displays; served as manager of other summer workers during owner's absence.

### A Large Number of Jobs
EMPLOYMENT: Recent Hospitality Industry Experience: Affiliated with four upscale hotel/restaurant complexes (September 2001–February 2004), where I worked part- and full-time as a waiter, bartender, disc jockey, and bookkeeper to produce income for college.

### Several Positions with the Same Employer
EMPLOYMENT: Coca-Cola Bottling Co., Burlington, Vermont, 2001–2004. In four years, I received three promotions, each with increased pay and responsibility.

*Summer Sales Coordinator:* Promoted to hire, train, and direct efforts of add-on staff of fifteen college-age route salespeople hired to meet summer peak demand for product.

*Sales Administrator:* Promoted to run home office sales desk, managing accounts and associated delivery schedules for professional sales force of ten people. Intensive phone work, daily interaction with all personnel, and strong knowledge of product line required.

*Route Salesperson:* Summer employment to travel and tourism industry sites that use Coke products. Met specific schedule demands, used good communication skills with wide variety of customers, and demonstrated strong selling skills. Named salesperson of the month for July and August of that year.

## Questions Résumé Writers Often Ask

### How Far Back Should I Go in Terms of Listing Past Jobs?

Usually, listing three or four jobs should suffice. If you did something back in high school that has a bearing on your future aspirations for employment, by all means list the job. As you progress through your college career, high school jobs will be replaced on the résumé by college employment.

### Should I Differentiate Between Paid and Nonpaid Employment?

Most employers are not initially concerned about how much you were paid. They are anxious to know how much responsibility you held in your past employment. There is no need to specify that your work was as a volunteer if you had significant responsibilities.

### How Should I Represent My Accomplishments or Work-Related Responsibilities?

Succinctly, but fully. In other words, give the employer enough information to arouse curiosity but not so much detail that you leave nothing to the imagination. Besides, some jobs merit more lengthy explanations than others. Be sure to convey any information that can give an employer a better understanding of the depth of your involvement at work. Did you supervise others? How many? Did your efforts result in a more efficient operation? How much did you increase efficiency? Did you handle a budget? How much? Were you promoted in a short time? Did you work two jobs at once or fifteen hours per week after high school? Where appropriate, quantify.

### Should the Work Section Always Follow the Education Section on the Résumé?

Always lead with your strengths. If your education closely relates to the employment you now seek, put this section after the objective. If your education does not closely relate but you have a surplus of good work experiences, consider reversing the order of your sections to lead with employment, followed by education.

### How Should I Present My Activities, Honors, Awards, Professional Societies, and Affiliations?

This section of the résumé can add valuable information for an employer to consider if used correctly. The rule of thumb for information in this section is to include only those activities that are in some way relevant to the objective stated on your résumé. If you can draw a valid connection between your activities and your objective, include them; if not, leave them out.

Professional affiliations and honors should all be listed; especially important are those related to your job objective. Social clubs and activities need not be a part of your résumé unless you hold a significant office or you are looking for a position related to your membership. Be aware that most prospective employers' principal concerns are related to your employability, not your social life. If you have any, publications can be included as an addendum to your résumé.

### How Should I Handle References?

The use of references is considered a part of the interview process, and they should never be listed on a résumé. You would always provide references to a potential employer if requested to, so it is not even necessary to include this section on the résumé if space does not permit. If space is available, it is acceptable to include the following statement:

- REFERENCES:
  Furnished upon request.

## The Functional Résumé

The functional résumé departs from a chronological résumé in that it organizes information by specific accomplishments in various settings: previous jobs, volunteer work, associations, and so forth. This type of résumé permits you to stress the substance of your experiences rather than the position titles you have held. You should consider using a functional résumé if you have held a series of similar jobs that relied on the same skills or abilities. There are many good books in which you can find examples of functional résumés, including *How to Write a Winning Resume* or *Resumes Made Easy*.

# The Targeted Résumé

The targeted résumé focuses on specific work-related capabilities you can bring to a given position within an organization. Past achievements are listed to highlight your capabilities and the work history section is abbreviated.

# Digital Résumés

Today's employers have to manage an enormous number of résumés. One of the most frequent complaints the writers of this series hear from students is the failure of employers to even acknowledge the receipt of a résumé and cover letter. Frequently, the reason for this poor response or nonresponse is the volume of applications received for every job. In an attempt to better manage the considerable labor investment involved in processing large numbers of résumés, many employers are requiring digital submission of résumés. There are two types of digital résumés: those that can be e-mailed or posted to a website, called *electronic résumés*, and those that can be "read" by a computer, commonly called *scannable résumés*. Though the format may be a bit different from the traditional "paper" résumé, the goal of both types of digital résumés is the same—to get you an interview! These résumés must be designed to be "technologically friendly." What that basically means to you is that they should be free of graphics and fancy formatting. (See Exhibit 2.2.)

### Electronic Résumés

Sometimes referred to as plain-text résumés, electronic résumés are designed to be e-mailed to an employer or posted to one of many commercial Internet databases such as CareerMosaic.com, America's Job Bank (ajb.dni.us), or Monster.com.

Some technical considerations:

- Electronic résumés must be written in American Standard Code for Information Interchange (ASCII), which is simply a plain-text format. These characters are universally recognized so that every computer can accurately read and understand them. To create an ASCII file of your current résumé, open your document, then save it as a text or ASCII file. This will eliminate all formatting. Edit as needed using your computer's text editor application.

Exhibit 2.2
## DIGITAL RÉSUMÉ

ANN PARKER
3400 El Camino Real
Boca Raton, FL 33432
561/555-7890
aparker@site.com

Put your name at the
top on its own line.

Put your phone number
on its own line.

### KEYWORD SUMMARY
Management accountant
Health care
Information systems design
Workplace communications
Internal auditing
Professional writing

Keywords make your
résumé easier to find in
a database.

Use a standard-width
typeface.

### EXPERIENCE
* Internship. 2003 to present; Motorola Corporation.
Assist Associate Financial Director, examine
financial records, and write reports. Projects
portfolio available.
* Summer Work-Study Program. 2001-2003;
Boca Raton Community Hospital. Bookkeeping
Department. Assisted with payroll and withholding
tax deductions.

Use a space between
asterisk and text.

No line should exceed
sixty-five characters.

### COMMUNITY SERVICE
* Volunteer. Medical Records Department, North
Broward General Hospital.
* Intake Processor. Student Red Cross Blood Drive,
Florida Atlantic University.

Capitalize letters to
emphasize headings.

End each line by
hitting the ENTER
(or RETURN) key.

- Use a standard-width typeface. Courier is a good choice because it is the font associated with ASCII in most systems.
- Use a font size of 11 to 14 points. A 12-point font is considered standard.
- Your margin should be left-justified.
- Do not exceed sixty-five characters per line because the word-wrap function doesn't operate in ASCII.
- Do not use boldface, italics, underlining, bullets, or various font sizes. Instead, use asterisks, plus signs, or all capital letters when you want to emphasize something.
- Avoid graphics and shading.
- Use as many "keywords" as you possibly can. These are words or phrases usually relating to skills or experience that either are specifically used in the job announcement or are popular buzzwords in the industry.
- Minimize abbreviations.
- Your name should be the first line of text.
- Conduct a "test run" by e-mailing your résumé to yourself and a friend before you send it to the employer. See how it transmits, and make any changes you need to. Continue to test it until it's exactly how you want it to look.
- Unless an employer specifically requests that you send the résumé in the form of an attachment, don't. Employers can encounter problems opening a document as an attachment, and there are always viruses to consider.
- Don't forget your cover letter. Send it along with your résumé as a single message.

## Scannable Résumés

Some companies are relying on technology to narrow the candidate pool for available job openings. Electronic Applicant Tracking uses imaging to scan, sort, and store résumé elements in a database. Then, through OCR (Optical Character Recognition) software, the computer scans the résumés for keywords and phrases. To have the best chance at getting an interview, you want to increase the number of "hits"—matches of your skills, abilities, experience, and education to those the computer is scanning for—your résumé will get. You can see how critical using the right keywords is for this type of résumé.

Technical considerations include:

- Again, do not use boldface (newer systems may read this OK, but many older ones won't), italics, underlining, bullets, shading, graphics, or multiple font sizes. Instead, for emphasis, use asterisks, plus signs, or all capital letters. Minimize abbreviations.
- Use a popular typeface such as Courier, Helvetica, Ariel, or Palatino. Avoid decorative fonts.
- Font size should be between 11 and 14 points.
- Do not compress the spacing between letters.
- Use horizontal and vertical lines sparingly; the computer may misread them as the letters *L* or *I*.
- Left-justify the text.
- Do not use parentheses or brackets around telephone numbers, and be sure your phone number is on its own line of text.
- Your name should be the first line of text and on its own line. If your résumé is longer than one page, be sure to put your name on the top of all pages.
- Use a traditional résumé structure. The chronological format may work best.
- Use nouns that are skill-focused, such as *management*, *writer*, and *programming*. This is different from traditional paper résumés, which use action-oriented verbs.
- Laser printers produce the finest copies. Avoid dot-matrix printers.
- Use standard, light-colored paper with text on one side only. Since the higher the contrast, the better, your best choice is black ink on white paper.
- Always send original copies. If you must fax, set the fax on fine mode, not standard.
- Do not staple or fold your résumé. This can confuse the computer.
- Before you send your scannable résumé, be certain the employer uses this technology. If you can't determine this, you may want to send two versions (scannable and traditional) to be sure your résumé gets considered.

## Résumé Production and Other Tips

An ink-jet printer is the preferred option for printing your résumé. Begin by printing just a few copies. You may find a small error or you may simply want to make some changes, and it is less frustrating and less expensive if you print in small batches.

Résumé paper color should be carefully chosen. You should consider the types of employers who will receive your résumé and the types of positions for which you are applying. Use white or ivory paper for traditional or conservative employers or for higher-level positions.

Black ink on sharp, white paper can be harsh on the reader's eyes. Think about an ivory or cream paper that will provide less contrast and be easier to read. Pink, green, and blue tints should generally be avoided.

Many résumé writers buy packages of matching envelopes and cover sheet stationery that, although not absolutely necessary, help convey a professional impression.

If you'll be producing many cover letters at home, be sure you have high-quality printing equipment. Learn standard envelope formats for business, and retain a copy of every cover letter you send out. You can use the copies to take notes of any telephone conversations that may occur.

If attending a job fair, either carry a briefcase or place your résumé in a nicely covered legal-size pad holder.

## The Cover Letter

The cover letter provides you with the opportunity to tailor your résumé by telling the prospective employer how you can be a benefit to the organization. It allows you to highlight aspects of your background that are not already discussed in your résumé and that might be especially relevant to the organization you are contacting or to the position you are seeking. Every résumé should have a cover letter enclosed when you send it out. Unlike the résumé, which may be mass-produced, a cover letter is most effective when it is individually prepared and focused on the particular requirements of the organization in question.

A good cover letter should supplement the résumé and motivate the reader to review the résumé. The format shown in Exhibit 2.3 (see page 34) is only a suggestion to help you decide what information to include in a cover letter.

Begin the cover letter with your street address six lines down from the top. Leave three to five lines between the date and the name of the person to whom you are addressing the cover letter. Make sure you leave one blank line between the salutation and the body of the letter and between paragraphs. After typing "Sincerely," leave four blank lines and type your name. This should leave plenty of room for your signature. A sample cover letter is shown in Exhibit 2.4 on page 35.

The following guidelines will help you write good cover letters:

1. Be sure to type your letter neatly; ensure there are no misspellings.
2. Avoid unusual typefaces, such as script.
3. Address the letter to an individual, using the person's name and title. To obtain this information, call the company. If answering a blind newspaper advertisement, address the letter "To Whom It May Concern" or omit the salutation.
4. Be sure your cover letter directly indicates the position you are applying for and tells why you are qualified to fill it.
5. Send the original letter, not a photocopy, with your résumé. Keep a copy for your records.
6. Make your cover letter no more than one page.
7. Include a phone number where you can be reached.
8. Avoid trite language and have someone read the letter over to react to its tone, content, and mechanics.
9. For your own information, record the date you send out each letter and résumé.

Exhibit 2.3
## COVER LETTER FORMAT

Your Street Address
Your Town, State, Zip
Phone Number
Fax Number
E-mail

Date

Name
Title
Organization
Address

Dear _____:

*First Paragraph.* In this paragraph state the reason for the letter, name the specific position or type of work you are applying for, and indicate from which resource (career services office, website, newspaper, contact, employment service) you learned of this opening. The first paragraph can also be used to inquire about future openings.

*Second Paragraph.* Indicate why you are interested in this position, the company, or its products or services and what you can do for the employer. If you are a recent graduate, explain how your academic background makes you a qualified candidate. Try not to repeat the same information found in the résumé.

*Third Paragraph.* Refer the reader to the enclosed résumé for more detailed information.

*Fourth Paragraph.* In this paragraph say what you will do to follow up on your letter. For example, state that you will call by a certain date to set up an interview or to find out if the company will be recruiting in your area. Finish by indicating your willingness to answer any questions the recipient may have. Be sure you have provided your phone number.

Sincerely,

*Type your name*
Enclosure

Exhibit 2.4
## SAMPLE COVER LETTER

229 Kelton Street #4
Brighton, MA 02135
(617) 555-3333
Jdust@xxx.com

May 10, 2005

Diane Irving
Director of Personnel
Sterling Museum
65 The Fenway
Boston, MA 02115

Dear Ms. Irving:

In June 2005, I will graduate from Boston University with a bachelor's degree in business management with a concentration in accounting. I read of your opening for an assistant management accountant in *The Globe* on Sunday, May 9, 2005, and I am very interested in the possibilities it offers. I am writing to explore the opportunity for employment with your museum. The ad indicated that you are looking for creative team players with good communication skills as well as quantitative skills and management accounting experience. I believe I possess those qualities. While interning at the Boston Museum of Fine Arts, I learned the ins and outs of the financial workings of a major museum, including the importance of teamwork.

In addition to the various accounting courses in my academic program, I studied art history (my first love), museum studies, and computer science, including the use of spreadsheets and databases. These courses helped me to become familiar with the inner workings of museums and their collections and to familiarize myself with a variety of computer accounting systems. I believe that this experience, coupled with my enthusiasm for working in an art museum environment, will help me to represent Sterling Museum in a professional and competent manner.

*continued*

As you will see in my enclosed résumé, I worked at the Museum of Fine Arts for a total of three years, both in the finance office and under the direction of the collections manager for eighteenth-century European art. These placements provided me with experience tracking both artwork and finances and allowed me to see how both offices function cooperatively.

I would like to meet with you to discuss how my education and experience would be consistent with your needs. I will contact your office next week to discuss the possibility of an interview. In the meantime, if you have any questions or require additional information, please contact me by phone at (617) 555-3333 or via e-mail at Jdust@xxx.com.

Sincerely,

Jane Dustin

Enclosure

# 3

# Researching Careers and Networking

One common question a career counselor encounters is "What can I do with my degree?" Accounting majors have narrowed their interests more than most liberal arts graduates, but it is still difficult to define all their choices. Accounting majors might know the type of accounting work they want to do—income tax returns or auditing, public or private, government or corporate—but they could be unsure of the various job settings in which work is available and satisfying. The job search may be daunting at first—almost every type of service, industry, or institution requires the services of a professional accountant. Would you fit in more comfortably at a large corporation, a small private business, a not-for-profit entity, a hospital, an educational institution, a local government agency, or any number of other settings? The choices really are limitless.

## What Do They Call the Job You Want?

One reason for confusion is perhaps a mistaken assumption that a college education provides job training. In most cases it does not. Of course, applied fields such as engineering, management, or education provide specific skills for the workplace as well as an education. Regardless, your overall college education exposes you to numerous fields of study and teaches you quantitative reasoning, critical thinking, writing, and speaking, all of which can be successfully applied to a number of different job fields. But it still remains up to you to choose a job field and to learn how to articulate the benefits of your education in a way the employer will appreciate.

## Collect Job Titles

The world of employment is a complex place, so you need to become a bit of an explorer and adventurer and be willing to try a variety of techniques to develop a list of possible occupations that might use your talents and education. You might find computerized interest inventories, reference books and other sources, and classified ads helpful in this respect. Once you have a list of possibilities that you are interested in and qualified for, you can move on to find out what kinds of organizations have these job titles.

*Computerized Interest Inventories.* One way to begin collecting job titles is to identify a number of jobs that call for your degree and the particular skills and interests you identified as part of the self-assessment process. There are excellent interactive career-guidance programs on the market to help you produce such selected lists of possible job titles. Most of these are available at colleges and at some larger town and city libraries. Two of the industry leaders are *CHOICES* and *DISCOVER*. Both allow you to enter interests, values, educational background, and other information to produce lists of possible occupations and industries. Each of the resources listed here will produce different job title lists. Some job titles will appear again and again, while others will be unique to a particular source. Investigate all of them!

*Reference Sources.* Books on the market that may be available through your local library or career counseling office also suggest various occupations related to specific majors. The following are only a few of the many good books on the market: *The College Board Guide to 150 Popular College Majors* and *College Majors and Careers: A Resource Guide for Effective Life Planning* both by Paul Phifer, and *Kaplan's What to Study: 101 Fields in a Flash*. All of these books list possible job titles within the academic major.

---

Not every employer seeking to hire someone with an accounting degree may be equally desirable to you. Employment environments can vary considerably from one employer to another. An accountant wanting to work in auditing could do so in a large corporation, a small firm within a corporation, a private concern, the government, a financial institution, or even a hospital. Each of these environments presents a different corporate culture with associated norms in the pace of work, the subject matter of interest, and the backgrounds of its employees. Although the job titles may be the same, not all locations may present the same fit for you.

If you majored in accounting and enjoyed the exacting, detailed work you did as part of your studies and if you have developed some strong investigative skills, you might naturally think about forensic accounting. But accounting majors with these same skills and interests might go on to teach others their skills or work as internal auditors. Each of these job titles can also be found in a number of different settings.

---

Each job title deserves your consideration. Like removing the layers of an onion, the search for job titles can go on and on! As you spend time doing this activity, you are actually learning more about the value of your degree. What's important in your search at this point is not to become critical or selective but rather to develop as long a list of possibilities as you can. Every source used will help you add new and potentially exciting jobs to your growing list.

**Classified Ads.** It has been well publicized that the classified ad section of the newspaper represents only a small fraction of the current job market. Nevertheless, the weekly classified ads can be a great help to you in your search. Although they may not be the best place to look for a job, they can teach you a lot about the job market. Classified ads provide a good education in job descriptions, duties, responsibilities, and qualifications. In addition, they provide insight into which industries are actively recruiting and some indication of the area's employment market. This is particularly helpful when seeking a position in a specific geographic area and/or a specific field. For your purposes, classified ads are a good source for job titles to add to your list.

Read the Sunday classified ads in a major market newspaper for several weeks in a row. Cut and paste all the ads that interest you and seem to call for something close to your education, skills, experience, and interests. Remember that classified ads are written for what an organization *hopes* to find; you don't have to meet absolutely every criterion. However, if certain requirements are stated as absolute minimums and you cannot meet them, it's best not to waste your time and that of the employer.

The weekly classified want ads exercise is important because these jobs are out in the marketplace. They truly exist, and people with your qualifications are being sought to apply. What's more, many of these advertisements describe the duties and responsibilities of the job advertised and give you a beginning sense of the challenges and opportunities such a position presents. Some will indicate salary, and that will be helpful as well. This information will better define the jobs for you and provide some good material for possible interviews in that field.

## Explore Job Descriptions

Once you've arrived at a solid list of possible job titles that interest you and for which you believe you are somewhat qualified, it's a good idea to do some research on each of these jobs. The preeminent source for such job information is the *Dictionary of Occupational Titles*, or *DOT* (wave.net/upg/immigration/dot_index.html). This directory lists every conceivable job and provides excellent up-to-date information on duties and responsibilities, interactions with associates, and day-to-day assignments and tasks. These descriptions provide a thorough job analysis, but they do not consider the possible employers or the environments in which a job may be performed. So, although a position as public relations officer may be well defined in terms of duties and responsibilities, it does not explain the differences in doing public relations work in a college or a hospital or a factory or a bank. You will need to look somewhere else for work settings.

## Learn More About Possible Work Settings

After reading some job descriptions, you may choose to edit and revise your list of job titles once again, discarding those you feel are not suitable and keeping those that continue to hold your interest. Or you may wish to keep your list intact and see where these jobs may be located. For example, if you are interested in public relations and you appear to have those skills and the requisite education, you'll want to know what organizations do public relations. How can you find that out? How much income does someone in public relations make a year and what is the employment potential for the field of public relations?

To answer these and many other questions about your list of job titles, we recommend you try any of the following resources: *Careers Encyclopedia*, the professional societies and resources found throughout this book, *College to Career: The Guide to Job Opportunities*, and the *Occupational Outlook Handbook* (http://stats.bls.gov/ocohome.htm). Each of these resources, in a different way, will help to put the job titles you have selected into an employer context. Perhaps the most extensive discussion is found in the *Occupational Outlook Handbook*, which gives a thorough presentation of the nature of the work, the working conditions, employment statistics, training, other qualifications, and advancement possibilities as well as job outlook and earnings. Related occupations are also detailed, and a select bibliography is provided to help you find additional information.

Continuing with our public relations example, your search through these reference materials would teach you that the public relations jobs you find attractive are available in larger hospitals, financial institutions, most corporations (both consumer goods and industrial goods), media organizations, and colleges and universities.

# Networking

Networking is the process of deliberately establishing relationships to get career-related information or to alert potential employers that you are available for work. Networking is critically important to today's job seeker for two reasons: it will help you get the information you need, and it can help you find out about *all* of the available jobs.

### Get the Information You Need

Networkers will review your résumé and give you feedback on its effectiveness. They will talk about the job you are looking for and give you a candid appraisal of how they see your strengths and weaknesses. If they have a good sense of the industry or the employment sector for that job, you'll get their feelings on future trends in the industry as well. Some networkers will be very forthcoming about salaries, job-hunting techniques, and suggestions for your job search strategy. Many have been known to place calls right from the interview desk to friends and associates who might be interested in you. Each networker will make his or her own contribution, and each will be valuable.

Because organizations must evolve to adapt to current global market needs, the information provided by decision makers within various organizations will be critical to your success as a new job market entrant. For example, you might learn about the concept of virtual organizations from a networker. Virtual organizations coordinate economic activity to deliver value to customers by using resources outside the traditional boundaries of the organization. This concept is being discussed and implemented by chief executive officers of many organizations, including Ford Motor, Dell, and IBM. Networking can help you find out about this and other trends currently affecting the industries under your consideration.

### Find Out About All of the Available Jobs

Not every job that is available at this very moment is advertised for potential applicants to see. This is called the *hidden job market*. Only 15 to 20 percent of all jobs are formally advertised, which means that 80 to 85 percent of available jobs do not appear in published channels. Networking will help you become more knowledgeable about all the employment opportunities available during your job search period.

Although someone you might talk to today doesn't know of any openings within his or her organization, tomorrow or next week or next month an opening may occur. If you've taken the time to show an interest in and knowledge of their organization, if you've shown the company representative how you can help achieve organizational goals and that you can fit into the organization, you'll be one of the first candidates considered for the position.

### Networking: A Proactive Approach

Networking is a proactive rather than a reactive approach. You, as a job seeker, are expected to initiate a certain level of activity on your own behalf; you cannot afford to simply respond to jobs listed in the newspaper. Being proactive means building a network of contacts that includes informed and interested decision makers who will provide you with up-to-date knowledge of the current job market and increase your chances of finding out about employment opportunities appropriate for your interests, experience, and level of education. An old axiom of networking says, "You are only two phone calls away from the information you need." In other words, by talking to enough people, you will quickly come across someone who can offer you help.

# Preparing to Network

In deliberately establishing relationships, maximize your efforts by organizing your approach. Five specific areas in which you can organize your efforts include reviewing your self-assessment, reviewing your research on job sites and organizations, deciding who it is you want to talk to, keeping track of all your efforts, and creating your self-promotion tools.

### Review Your Self-Assessment

Your self-assessment is as important a tool in preparing to network as it has been in other aspects of your job search. You have carefully evaluated your personal traits, personal values, economic needs, longer-term goals, skill base, preferred skills, and underdeveloped skills. During the networking process you will be called upon to communicate what you know about yourself and relate it to the information or job you seek. Be sure to review the exercises that you completed in the self-assessment section of this book in preparation for networking. We've explained that you need to assess what skills you have acquired from your major that are of general value to an employer and to be ready to express those in ways employers can appreciate as useful in their own organizations.

## Review Research on Job Sites and Organizations

In addition, individuals assisting you will expect that you'll have at least some background information on the occupation or industry of interest to you. Refer to the appropriate sections of this book and other relevant publications to acquire the background information necessary for effective networking. They'll explain how to identify not only the job titles that might be of interest to you but also what kinds of organizations employ people to do that job. You will develop some sense of working conditions and expectations about duties and responsibilities—all of which will be of help in your networking interviews.

## Decide Who It Is You Want to Talk To

Networking cannot begin until you decide who it is that you want to talk to and, in general, what type of information you hope to gain from your contacts. Once you know this, it's time to begin developing a list of contacts. Five useful sources for locating contacts are described here.

*College Alumni Network.* Most colleges and universities have created a formal network of alumni and friends of the institution who are particularly interested in helping currently enrolled students and graduates of their alma mater gain employment-related information.

It is usually a simple process to make use of an alumni network. Visit your college's website and locate the alumni office and/or your career center. Either or both sites will have information about your school's alumni network. You'll be provided with information on shadowing experiences, geographic information, or those alumni offering job referrals. If you don't find what you're looking for, don't hesitate to phone or e-mail your career center and ask what they can do to help you connect with an alum.

Alumni networkers may provide some combination of the following services: day-long shadowing experiences, telephone interviews, in-person interviews, information on relocating to given geographic areas, internship information, suggestions on graduate school study, and job vacancy notices.

**Present and Former Supervisors.** If you believe you are on good terms with present or former job supervisors, they may be an excellent resource for providing information or directing you to appropriate resources that would have information related to your current interests and needs. Additionally, these supervisors probably belong to professional organizations that they might be willing to utilize to get information for you.

**Employers in Your Area.** Although you may be interested in working in a geographic location different from the one where you currently reside, don't overlook the value of the knowledge and contacts those around you are able to provide. Use the local telephone directory and newspaper to identify the types of organizations you are thinking of working for or professionals who have the kinds of jobs you are interested in. Recently, a call made to a local hospital's financial administrator for information on working in health-care financial administration yielded more pertinent information on training seminars, regional professional organizations, and potential employment sites than a national organization was willing to provide.

**Employers in Geographic Areas Where You Hope to Work.** If you are thinking about relocating, identifying prospective employers or informational contacts in the new location will be critical to your success. Here are some tips for online searching. First, use a "metasearch" engine to get the most out of your search. Metasearch engines combine several engines into one powerful tool. We frequently use dogpile.com and metasearch.com for this purpose. Try using the city and state as your keywords in a search. *New Haven, Connecticut* will bring you to the city's website with links to the chamber of commerce, member businesses, and other valuable resources. By using looksmart.com you can locate newspapers in any area, and they, too, can provide valuable insight before you relocate. Of course, both dogpile and metasearch can lead you to yellow and white page directories in areas you are considering.

**Professional Associations and Organizations.** Professional associations and organizations can provide valuable information in several areas: career paths that you might not have considered, qualifications relating to those career choices, publications that list current job openings, and workshops or seminars that will enhance your professional knowledge and skills. They can also be excellent sources for background information on given industries: their health, current problems, and future challenges.

There are several excellent resources available to help you locate professional associations and organizations that would have information to meet your needs. Two especially useful publications are the *Encyclopedia of Associations* and *National Trade and Professional Associations of the United States*.

### Keep Track of All Your Efforts

It can be difficult, almost impossible, to remember all the details related to each contact you make during the networking process, so you will want to develop a record-keeping system that works for you. Formalize this process by using your computer to keep a record of the people and organizations you want to contact. You can simply record the contact's name, address, and telephone number, and what information you hope to gain.

You could record this as a simple Word document and you could still use the "Find" function if you were trying to locate some data and could only recall the firm's name or the contact's name. If you're comfortable with database management and you have some database software on your computer, then you can put information at your fingertips even if you have only the zip code! The point here is not technological sophistication but good record keeping.

Once you have created this initial list, it will be helpful to keep more detailed information as you begin to actually make the contacts. Those details should include complete contact information, the date and content of each contact, names and information for additional networkers, and required follow-up. Don't forget to send a letter thanking your contact for his or her time! Your contact will appreciate your recall of details of your meetings and conversations, and the information will help you to focus your networking efforts.

### Create Your Self-Promotion Tools

There are two types of promotional tools that are used in the networking process. The first is a résumé and cover letter, and the second is a one-minute "infomercial," which may be given over the telephone or in person.

Techniques for writing an effective résumé and cover letter are discussed in Chapter 2. Once you have reviewed that material and prepared these important documents, you will have created one of your self-promotion tools.

The one-minute infomercial will demand that you begin tying your interests, abilities, and skills to the people or organizations you want to network with. Think about your goal for making the contact to help you understand what you should say about yourself. You should be able to express yourself easily and convincingly. If, for example, you are contacting an alumnus of your institution to obtain the names of possible employment sites in a distant city, be prepared to discuss why you are interested in moving to that location, the types of jobs you are interested in, and the skills and abilities you possess that will make you a qualified candidate.

To create a meaningful one-minute infomercial, write it out, practice it as if it will be a spoken presentation, rewrite it, and practice it again if necessary until expressing yourself comes easily and is convincing.

Here's a simplified example of an infomercial for use over the telephone:

---

Hello, Mr. Pollard? My name is Sherry Douglas. I am a recent graduate of State College, and I wish to enter the health-care field in accounting. I was an accounting major and feel confident I have many of the skills I understand are valued for accountants in health care. I have a strong quantitative background, with good investigative and computer skills. What's more, I have excellent interpersonal skills and work well under pressure. I understand these are valuable traits in this line of work!

Mr. Pollard, I'm calling you because I still need more information about accounting in the health-care field. I'm hoping you'll have the time to sit down with me for about half an hour and discuss your perspective on accounting careers. There are so many possible places to get into accounting, and I am seeking some advice on which of those settings might be the best bet for my particular combination of skills and experience.

Would you be willing to do that for me? I would greatly appreciate it. I am available most mornings, if that time is convenient for you.

---

It very well may happen that your employer contact wishes you to communicate by e-mail. The infomercial quoted above could easily be rewritten for an e-mail message. You should "cut and paste" your résumé right into the e-mail text itself.

Other effective self-promotion tools include portfolios for those in the arts, writing professions, or teaching. Portfolios show examples of work, photographs of projects or classroom activities, or certificates and credentials that are job related. There may not be an opportunity to use the portfolio during an interview, and it is not something that should be left with the organization. It is designed to be explained and displayed by the creator. However, during some networking meetings, there may be an opportunity to illustrate a point or strengthen a qualification by exhibiting the portfolio.

## Beginning the Networking Process

### Set the Tone for Your Communications

It can be useful to establish "tone words" for any communications you embark upon. Before making your first telephone call or writing your first letter, decide what you want the person to think of you. If you are networking to try to obtain a job, your tone words might include descriptors such as *genuine*, *informed*, and *self-knowledgeable*. When you're trying to acquire information, your tone words may have a slightly different focus, such as *courteous*, *organized*, *focused*, and *well-spoken*. Use the tone words you establish for your contacts to guide you through the networking process.

### Honestly Express Your Intentions

When contacting individuals, it is important to be honest about your reasons for making the contact. Establish your purpose in your own mind and be able and ready to articulate it concisely. Determine an initial agenda, whether it be informational questioning or self-promotion, present it to your contact, and be ready to respond immediately. If you don't adequately prepare before initiating your overture, you may find yourself at a disadvantage if you're asked to immediately begin your informational interview or self-promotion during the first phone conversation or visit.

### Start Networking Within Your Circle of Confidence

Once you have organized your approach—by utilizing specific researching methods, creating a system for keeping track of the people you will contact, and developing effective self-promotion tools—you are ready to begin networking. The best way to begin networking is by talking with a group of people you trust and feel comfortable with. This group is usually made up of your family, friends, and career counselors. No matter who is in this inner circle, they will have a special interest in seeing you succeed in your job search. In addition, because they will be easy to talk to, you should try taking some risks in terms of practicing your information-seeking approach. Gain confidence in talking about the strengths you bring to an organization and the underdeveloped skills you feel hinder your candidacy. Be sure to review the section on self-assessment for tips on approaching each of these areas. Ask for critical but constructive feedback from the people in your circle of confidence on the letters you write and the one-minute infomercial you have developed. Evaluate whether you want to make the changes they suggest, then practice the changes on others within this circle.

## Stretch the Boundaries of Your Networking Circle of Confidence

Once you have refined the promotional tools you will use to accomplish your networking goals, you will want to make additional contacts. Because you will not know most of these people, it will be a less comfortable activity to undertake. The practice that you gained with your inner circle of trusted friends should have prepared you to now move outside of that comfort zone.

It is said that any information a person needs is only two phone calls away, but the information cannot be gained until you (1) make a reasonable guess about who might have the information you need and (2) pick up the telephone to make the call. Using your network list that includes alumni, instructors, supervisors, employers, and associations, you can begin preparing your list of questions that will allow you to get the information you need.

## Prepare the Questions You Want to Ask

Networkers can provide you with the insider's perspective on any given field and you can ask them questions that you might not want to ask in an interview. For example, you can ask them to describe the more repetitious or mundane parts of the job or ask them for a realistic idea of salary expectations. Be sure to prepare your questions ahead of time so that you are organized and efficient.

## Be Prepared to Answer Some Questions

To communicate effectively, you must anticipate questions that will be asked of you by the networkers you contact. Revisit the self-assessment process you undertook and the research you've done so that you can effortlessly respond to questions about your short- and long-term goals and the kinds of jobs you are most interested in pursuing.

### General Networking Tips

*Make Every Contact Count.* Setting the tone for each interaction is critical. Approaches that will help you communicate in an effective way include politeness, being appreciative of time provided to you, and being prepared and thorough. Remember, *everyone* within an organization has a circle of influence, so be prepared to interact effectively with each person you encounter in the networking process, including secretarial and support staff. Many information or job seekers have thwarted their own efforts by being rude to some individuals they encountered as they networked because they made the incorrect assumption that certain persons were unimportant.

Sometimes your contacts may be surprised at their ability to help you. After meeting and talking with you, they might think they have not offered much in the way of help. A day or two later, however, they may make a contact that would be useful to you and refer you to that person.

*With Each Contact, Widen Your Circle of Networkers.* Always leave an informational interview with the names of at least two more people who can help you get the information or job that you are seeking. Don't be shy about asking for additional contacts; networking is all about increasing the number of people you can interact with to achieve your goals.

*Make Your Own Decisions.* As you talk with different people and get answers to the questions you pose, you may hear conflicting information or get conflicting suggestions. Your job is to listen to these "experts" and decide what information and which suggestions will help you achieve *your* goals. Only implement those suggestions that you believe will work for you.

## Shutting Down Your Network

As you achieve the goals that motivated your networking activity—getting the information you need or the job you want—the time will come to inactivate all or parts of your network. As you do, be sure to tell your primary supporters about your change in status. Call or write to each one of them and give them as many details about your new status as you feel is necessary to maintain a positive relationship.

Because a network takes on a life of its own, activity undertaken on your behalf will continue even after you cease your efforts. As you get calls or are contacted in some fashion, be sure to inform these networkers about your change in status, and thank them for assistance they have provided.

Information on the latest employment trends indicates that workers will change jobs or careers several times in their lifetime. Networking, then, will be a critical aspect in the span of your professional life. If you carefully and thoughtfully conduct your networking activities during your job search, you will have a solid foundation of experience when you need to network the next time around.

# Where Are These Jobs, Anyway?

Having a list of job titles that you've designed around your own career interests and skills is an excellent beginning. It means you've really thought about who you are and what you are presenting to the employment market. It has caused you to think seriously about the most appealing environments to work in, and you have identified some employer types that represent these environments.

The research and the thinking that you've done thus far will be used again and again. They will be helpful in writing your résumé and cover letters, in talking about yourself on the telephone to prospective employers, and in answering interview questions.

Now is a good time to begin to narrow the field of job titles and employment sites down to some specific employers to initiate the employment contact.

## Find Out Which Employers Hire People Like You

This section will provide tips, techniques, and specific resources for developing an actual list of specific employers that can be used to make contacts. It is only an outline that you must be prepared to tailor to your own particular needs and according to what you bring to the job search. Once again, it is important to communicate with others along the way exactly what you're looking for and what your goals are for the research you're doing. Librarians, employers, career counselors, friends, friends of friends, business contacts, and bookstore staff will all have helpful information on geographically specific and new resources to aid you in locating employers who'll hire you.

## Identify Information Resources

Your interview wardrobe and your new résumé might have put a dent in your wallet, but the resources you'll need to pursue your job search are available for free. The categories of information detailed here are not hard to find and are yours for the browsing.

Numerous resources described in this section will help you identify actual employers. Use all of them or any others that you identify as available in your geographic area. As you become experienced in this process, you'll quickly figure out which information sources are helpful and which are not. If you live in a rural area, a well-planned day trip to a major city that includes a college career office, a large college or city library, state and federal employment centers, a chamber of commerce office, and a well-stocked bookstore can produce valuable results.

There are many excellent resources available to help you identify actual job sites. They are categorized into employer directories (usually indexed by product lines and geographic location), geographically based directories (designed to highlight particular cities, regions, or states), career-specific directories (e.g., *Sports MarketPlace*, which lists tens of thousands of firms involved with sports), periodicals and newspapers, targeted job posting publications, and videos. This is by no means meant to be a complete treatment of resources but rather a starting point for identifying useful resources.

Working from the more general references to highly specific resources, we provide a basic list to help you begin your search. Many of these you'll find easily available. In some cases reference librarians and others will suggest even better materials for your particular situation. Start to create your own customized bibliography of job search references.

***Geographically Based Directories.*** The Job Bank series published by Bob Adams, Inc. (aip.com) contains detailed entries on each area's major employers, including business activity, address, phone number, and hiring contact name. Many listings specify educational backgrounds being sought in potential employees. Each volume contains a solid discussion of each city's or state's major employment sectors. Organizations are also indexed by industry. Job Bank volumes are available for the following places: Atlanta, Boston, Chicago, Dallas–Ft. Worth, Denver, Detroit, Florida, Houston, Los Angeles, Minneapolis, New York, Ohio, Philadelphia, San Francisco, Seattle, St. Louis, Washington, D.C., and other cities throughout the Northwest.

*National Job Bank* (careercity.com) lists employers in every state, along with contact names and commonly hired job categories. Included are many small companies often overlooked by other directories. Companies are also indexed by industry. This publication provides information on educational backgrounds sought and lists company benefits.

**Periodicals and Newspapers.** Several sources are available to help you locate which journals or magazines carry job advertisements in your field. Other resources help you identify opportunities in other parts of the country.

- *Where the Jobs Are: A Comprehensive Directory of 1200 Journals Listing Career Opportunities*
- *Corptech Fast 5000 Company Locator*
- *National Ad Search* (nationaladsearch.com)
- *The Federal Jobs Digest* (jobsfed.com) and *Federal Career Opportunities*
- *World Chamber of Commerce Directory* (chamberofcommerce.org)

This list is certainly not exhaustive; use it to begin your job search work.

**Targeted Job Posting Publications.** Although the resources that follow are national in scope, they are either targeted to one medium of contact (telephone), focused on specific types of jobs, or less comprehensive than the sources previously listed.

- Careers.org (careers.org/index.html)
- *The Job Hunter* (jobhunter.com)
- *Current Jobs for Graduates* (graduatejobs.com)
- *Environmental Opportunities* (ecojobs.com)
- *Y National Vacancy List* (ymca.net/employment/ymca_recruiting/jobright.htm)
- *ArtSEARCH*
- *Community Jobs*
- *National Association of Colleges and Employers: Job Choices series*
- *National Association of Colleges and Employers* (jobweb.com)

***Videos.*** You may be one of the many job seekers who likes to get information via a medium other than paper. Many career libraries, public libraries, and career centers in libraries carry an assortment of videos that will help you learn new techniques and get information helpful in the job search.

## Locate Information Resources

Throughout these introductory chapters, we have continually referred you to various websites for information on everything from job listings to career information. Using the Web gives you a mobility at your computer that you don't enjoy if you rely solely on books or newspapers or printed journals. Moreover, material on the Web, if the site is maintained, can be the most up-to-date information available.

You'll eventually identify the information resources that work best for you, but make certain you've covered the full range of resources before you begin to rely on a smaller list. Here's a short list of informational sites that many job seekers find helpful:

- Public and college libraries
- College career centers
- Bookstores
- The Internet
- Local and state government personnel offices
- Career/job fairs

Each one of these sites offers a collection of resources that will help you get the information you need.

As you meet and talk with service professionals at all these sites, be sure to let them know what you're doing. Inform them of your job search, what you've already accomplished, and what you're looking for. The more people who know you're job seeking, the greater the possibility that someone will have information or know someone who can help you along your way.

# 4

# Interviewing and Job Offer Considerations

Certainly, there can be no one part of the job search process more fraught with anxiety and worry than the interview. Yet seasoned job seekers welcome the interview and will often say, "Just get me an interview and I'm on my way!" They understand that the interview is crucial to the hiring process and equally crucial for them, as job candidates, to have the opportunity of a personal dialogue to add to what the employer may already have learned from the résumé, cover letter, and telephone conversations.

Believe it or not, the interview is to be welcomed, and even enjoyed! It is a perfect opportunity for you, the candidate, to sit down with an employer and express yourself and display who you are and what you want. Of course, it takes thought and planning and a little strategy; after all, it *is* a job interview! But it can be a positive, if not pleasant, experience and one you can look back on and feel confident about your performance and effort.

For many new job seekers, a job, any job, seems a wonderful thing. But seasoned interview veterans know that the job interview is an important step for both sides—the employer and the candidate—to see what each has to offer and whether there is going to be a "fit" of personalities, work styles, and attitudes. And it is this concept of balance in the interview, that both sides have important parts to play, that holds the key to success in mastering this aspect of the job search strategy.

Try to think of the interview as a conversation between two interested and equal partners. You both have important, even vital, information to deliver and to learn. Of course, there's no denying the employer has some leverage, especially in the initial interview for recruitment or any interview scheduled by the candidate and not the recruiter. That should not prevent the interviewee from seeking to play an equal part in what should be a fair exchange of information. Too often the untutored candidate allows the interview to become one-sided. The employer asks all the questions and the candidate simply responds. The ideal would be for two mutually interested parties to sit down and discuss possibilities for each. This is a conversation of significance, and it requires preparation, thought about the tone of the interview, and planning of the nature and details of the information to be exchanged.

## Preparing for the Interview

The length of most initial interviews is about thirty minutes. Given the brevity, the information that is exchanged ought to be important. The candidate should be delivering material that the employer cannot discover on the résumé, and in turn, the candidate should be learning things about the employer that he or she could not otherwise find out. After all, if you have only thirty minutes, why waste time on information that is already published? The information exchanged is more than just factual, and both sides will learn much from what they see of each other, as well. How the candidate looks, speaks, and acts are important to the employer. The employer's attention to the interview and awareness of the candidate's résumé, the setting, and the quality of information presented are important to the candidate.

Just as the employer has every right to be disappointed when a prospect is late for the interview, looks unkempt, and seems ill-prepared to answer fairly standard questions, the candidate may be disappointed with an interviewer who isn't ready for the meeting, hasn't learned the basic résumé facts, and is constantly interrupted by telephone calls. In either situation there's good reason to feel let down.

There are many elements to a successful interview, and some of them are not easy to describe or prepare for. Sometimes there is just a chemistry between interviewer and interviewee that brings out the best in both, and a good exchange takes place. But there is much the candidate can do to pave the way for success in terms of his or her résumé, personal appearance, goals, and interview strategy—each of which we will discuss. However, none of this preparation is as important as the time and thought the candidate gives to personal self-assessment.

### Self-Assessment
Neither a stunning résumé nor an expensive, well-tailored suit can compensate for candidates who do not know what they want, where they are going, or why they are interviewing with a particular employer. Self-assessment, the

process by which we begin to know and acknowledge our own particular blend of education, experiences, needs, and goals, is not something that can be sorted out the weekend before a major interview. Of all the elements of interview preparation, this one requires the longest lead time and cannot be faked.

Because the time allotted for most interviews is brief, it is all the more important for job candidates to understand and express succinctly why they are there and what they have to offer. This is not a time for undue modesty (or for braggadocio either); it is a time for a compelling, reasoned statement of why you feel that you and this employer might make a good match. It means you have to have thought about your skills, interests, and attributes; related those to your life experiences and your own history of challenges and opportunities; and determined what that indicates about your strengths, preferences, values, and areas needing further development.

If you need some assistance with self-assessment issues, refer to Chapter 1. Included are suggested exercises that can be done as needed, such as making up an experiential diary and extracting obvious strengths and weaknesses from past experiences. These simple assignments will help you look at past activities as collections of tasks with accompanying skills and responsibilities. Don't overlook your high school or college career office. Many offer personal counseling on self-assessment issues and may provide testing instruments such as the *Myers-Briggs Type Indicator (MBTI)*, the *Harrington-O'Shea Career Decision-Making System (CDM)*, the *Strong Interest Inventory (SII)*, or any other of a wide selection of assessment tools that can help you clarify some of these issues prior to the interview stage of your job search.

## The Résumé

Résumé preparation has been discussed in detail, and some basic examples were provided. In this section we want to concentrate on how best to use your résumé in the interview. In most cases the employer will have seen the résumé prior to the interview, and, in fact, it may well have been the quality of that résumé that secured the interview opportunity.

An interview is a conversation, however, and not an exercise in reading. So, if the employer hasn't seen your résumé and you have brought it along to the interview, wait until asked or until the end of the interview to offer it. Otherwise, you may find yourself staring at the back of your résumé and simply answering "yes" and "no" to a series of questions drawn from that document.

Sometimes an interviewer is not prepared and does not know or recall the contents of the résumé and may use the résumé to a greater or lesser degree as a "prompt" during the interview. It is for you to judge what that may indicate about the individual performing the interview or the employer. If your interviewer seems surprised by the scheduled meeting, relies on the résumé to an inordinate degree, and seems otherwise unfamiliar with your background, this lack of preparation for the hiring process could well be a symptom of general management disorganization or may simply be the result of poor planning on the part of one individual. It is your responsibility as a potential employee to be aware of these signals and make your decisions accordingly.

---

If you find that the interviewer is reading from your résumé rather than discussing the job with you, you can guide the interviewer back to the job dialogue by saying, "Mr. Davis, I would like to elaborate on the accounting experience I gained in an internship that is not detailed on my résumé." This strategy may give you an opportunity to convey more information about your strengths and weaknesses and will reengage the direction of your interview.

---

By all means, bring at least one copy of your résumé to the interview. Occasionally, at the close of an interview, an interviewer will express an interest in circulating a résumé to several departments, and you could then offer the copy you brought. Sometimes, an interview appointment provides an opportunity to meet others in the organization who may express an interest in you and your background, and it may be helpful to follow up with a copy of your résumé. Our best advice, however, is to keep it out of sight until needed or requested.

## Employer Information

Whether your interview is for graduate school admission, an overseas corporate position, or a position with a local company, it is important to know something about the employer or the organization. Keeping in mind that the interview is relatively brief and that you will hopefully have other interviews with other organizations, it is important to keep your research in proportion. If secondary interviews are called for, you will have additional time to do further research. For the first interview, it is helpful to know the organization's mission, goals, size, scope of operations, and so forth. Your research may uncover recent areas of challenge or particular successes that may help to fuel the interview. Use the "What Do They Call the Job You Want?" section of Chapter 3, your library, and your career or guidance office to help you locate this information in the most efficient way possible. Don't be shy in asking advice of these counseling and guidance professionals on how best to spend your preparation time. With some practice, you'll soon learn how much information is enough and which kinds of information are most useful to you.

## Interview Content

We've already discussed how it can help to think of the interview as an important conversation—one that, as with any conversation, you want to find pleasant and interesting and to leave you with a good feeling. But because this conversation is especially important, the information that's exchanged is critical to its success. What do you want them to know about you? What do you need to know about them? What interview technique do you need to particularly pay attention to? How do you want to manage the close of the interview? What steps will follow in the hiring process?

Except for the professional interviewer, most of us find interviewing stressful and anxiety-provoking. Developing a strategy before you begin interviewing will help you relieve some stress and anxiety. One particular strategy that has worked for many and may work for you is interviewing by objective. Before you interview, write down three to five goals you would like to achieve for that interview. They may be technique goals: smile a little more, have a firmer handshake, be sure to ask about the next stage in the interview process before leaving. They may be content-oriented goals: find out about the company's current challenges and opportunities; be sure to speak of your recent research, writing experiences, or foreign travel. Whatever your goals, jot down a few of them as goals for each interview.

Most people find that in trying to achieve these few goals, their interviewing technique becomes more organized and focused. After the interview, the most common question friends and family ask is "How did it go?" With this technique, you have an indication of whether you met *your* goals for the meeting, not just some vague idea of how it went. Chances are, if you accomplished what you wanted to, it improved the quality of the entire interview. As you continue to interview, you will want to revise your goals to continue improving your interview skills.

Now, add to the concept of the significant conversation the idea of a beginning, a middle, and a closing and you will have two thoughts that will give your interview a distinctive character. Be sure to make your introduction warm and cordial. Say your full name (and if it's a difficult-to-pronounce name, help the interviewer to pronounce it) and make certain you know your interviewer's name and how to pronounce it. Most interviews begin with some "soft talk" about the weather, chat about the candidate's trip to the interview site, or national events. This is done as a courtesy to relax both you and the interviewer, to get you talking, and to generally try to defuse the atmosphere of excessive tension. Try to be yourself, engage in the conversation, and don't try to second-guess the interviewer. This is simply what it appears to be—casual conversation.

Once you and the interviewer move on to exchange more serious information in the middle part of the interview, the two most important concerns become your ability to handle challenging questions and your success at asking meaningful ones. Interviewer questions will probably fall into one of three categories: personal assessment and career direction, academic assessment, and knowledge of the employer. Here are a few examples of questions in each category:

### Personal Assessment and Career Direction
1. What motivates you to put forth your best effort?
2. What do you consider to be your greatest strengths and weaknesses?
3. What qualifications do you have that make you think you will be successful in this career?

### Academic Assessment
1. What led you to choose your major?
2. What subjects did you like best and least? Why?
3. How has your college experience prepared you for this career?

### Knowledge of the Employer
1. What do you think it takes to be successful in an organization like ours?
2. In what ways do you think you can make a contribution to our organization?
3. Why did you choose to seek a position with this organization?

The interviewer wants a response to each question but is also gauging your enthusiasm, preparedness, and willingness to communicate. In each response you should provide some information about yourself that can be related to the employer's needs. A common mistake is to give too much information. Answer each question completely, but be careful not to run on too long with extensive details or examples.

## Questions About Underdeveloped Skills

Most employers interview people who have met some minimum criteria of education and experience. They interview candidates to see who they are, to learn what kind of personality they exhibit, and to get some sense of how this person might fit into the existing organization. It may be that you are asked about skills the employer hopes to find and that you have not documented. Maybe it's grant-writing experience, knowledge of the European political system, or a knowledge of the film world.

To questions about skills and experiences you don't have, answer honestly and forthrightly and try to offer some additional information about skills you do have. For example, perhaps the employer is disappointed you have no grant-writing experience. An honest answer may be as follows:

*No, unfortunately, I was never in a position to acquire those skills. I do understand something of the complexities of the grant-writing process and feel confident that my attention to detail, careful reading skills, and strong writing would make grants a wonderful challenge in a new job. I think I could get up on the learning curve quickly.*

The employer hears an honest admission of lack of experience but is reassured by some specific skill details that do relate to grant writing and a confident manner that suggests enthusiasm and interest in a challenge.

For many students, questions about their possible contribution to an employer's organization can prove challenging. Because your education has probably not included specific training for a job, you need to review your academic record and select capabilities you have developed in your major that an employer can appreciate. For example, perhaps you read well and can analyze and condense what you've read into smaller, more focused pieces. That could be valuable. Or maybe you did some serious research and you know you have valuable investigative skills. Your public speaking might be highly developed and you might use visual aids appropriately and effectively. Or maybe your skill at correspondence, memos, and messages is effective. Whatever it is, you must take it out of the academic context and put it into a new, employer-friendly context so your interviewer can best judge how you could help the organization.

Exhibiting knowledge of the organization will, without a doubt, show the interviewer that you are interested enough in the available position to have done some legwork in preparation for the interview. Remember, it is not necessary to know every detail of the organization's history but rather to have a general knowledge about why it is in business and how the industry is faring.

Sometime during the interview, generally after the midway point, you'll be asked if you have any questions for the interviewer. Your questions will tell the employer much about your attitude and your desire to understand the organization's expectations so you can compare them to your own strengths. The following are just a few questions you might want to ask:

1. What is the communication style of the organization? (meetings, memos, and so forth)
2. What would a typical day in this position be like for me?
3. What have been some of the interesting challenges and opportunities your organization has recently faced?

Most interviews draw to a natural closing point, so be careful not to prolong the discussion. At a signal from the interviewer, wind up your presentation, express your appreciation for the opportunity, and be sure to ask what the next stage in the process will be. When can you expect to hear from them? Will they be conducting second-tier interviews? If you are interested and haven't heard, would they mind a phone call? Be sure to collect a business card with the name and phone number of your interviewer. On your way out, you might have an opportunity to pick up organizational literature you haven't seen before.

With the right preparation—a thorough self-assessment, professional clothing, and employer information—you'll be able to set and achieve the goals you have established for the interview process.

# Interview Follow-Up

Quite often there is a considerable time lag between interviewing for a position and being hired or, in the case of the networker, between your phone call or letter to a possible contact and the opportunity of a meeting. This can be frustrating. "Why aren't they contacting me?" "I thought I'd get another interview, but no one has telephoned." "Am I out of the running?" You don't know what is happening.

## Consider the Differing Perspectives

Of course, there is another perspective—that of the networker or hiring organization. Organizations are complex, with multiple tasks that need to be accomplished each day. Hiring is a discrete activity that does not occur as frequently as other job assignments. The hiring process might have to take second place to other, more immediate organizational needs. Although it may be very important to you, and it is certainly ultimately significant to the employer, other issues such as fiscal management, planning and product development, employer vacation periods, or financial constraints may prevent an organization or individual within that organization from acting on your employment or your request for information as quickly as you or they would prefer.

## Use Your Communication Skills

Good communication is essential here to resolve any anxieties, and the responsibility is on you, the job or information seeker. Too many job seekers and networkers offer as an excuse that they don't want to "bother" the organization by writing letters or calling. Let us assure you here and now, once and for all, that if you are troubling an organization by over-communicating, someone will indicate that situation to you quite clearly. If not, you can only assume you are a worthwhile prospect and the employer appreciates being reminded of your availability and interest. Let's look at follow-up practices in the job interview process and the networking situation separately.

## Following Up on the Employment Interview

A brief thank-you note following an interview is an excellent and polite way to begin a series of follow-up communications with a potential employer with whom you have interviewed and want to remain in touch. It should be just that—a thank-you for a good meeting. If you failed to mention some fact or experience during your interview that you think might add to your candidacy, you may use this note to do that. However, this should be essentially a note whose overall tone is appreciative and, if appropriate, indicative of a continuing interest in pursuing any opportunity that may exist with that organization. It is one of the few pieces of business correspondence that may be handwritten, but always use plain, good-quality, standard-size paper.

If, however, at this point you are no longer interested in the employer, the thank-you note is an appropriate time to indicate that. You are under no obligation to identify any reason for not continuing to pursue employment with that organization, but if you are so inclined to indicate your professional reasons (pursuing other employers more akin to your interests, looking for greater income production than this employer can provide, a different geographic location), you certainly may. It should not be written with an eye to negotiation, for it will not be interpreted as such.

As part of your interview closing, you should have taken the initiative to establish lines of communication for continuing information about your candidacy. If you asked permission to telephone, wait a week following your thank-you note, then telephone your contact simply to inquire how things are progressing on your employment status. The feedback you receive here should be taken at face value. If your interviewer simply has no information, he or she will tell you so and indicate whether you should call again and when. Don't be discouraged if this should continue over some period of time.

If during this time something occurs that you think improves or changes your candidacy (some new qualification or experience you may have had), including any offers from other organizations, by all means telephone or write to inform the employer about this. In the case of an offer from a competing but less desirable or equally desirable organization, telephone your contact, explain what has happened, express your real interest in the organization, and inquire whether some determination on your employment might be made before you must respond to this other offer. An organization that is truly interested in you may be moved to make a decision about your candidacy. Equally possible is the scenario in which they are not yet ready to make a decision and so advise you to take the offer that has been presented. Again, you have no ethical alternative but to deal with the information presented in a straightforward manner.

When accepting other employment, be sure to contact any employers still actively considering you and inform them of your new job. Thank them graciously for their consideration. There are many other job seekers out there just like you who will benefit from having their candidacy improved when others bow out of the race. Who knows, you might at some future time have occasion to interact professionally with one of the organizations with which you sought employment. How embarrassing it would be to have someone remember you as the candidate who failed to notify them that you were taking a job elsewhere!

In all of your follow-up communications, keep good notes of whom you spoke with, when you called, and any instructions that were given about return communications. This will prevent any misunderstandings and provide you with good records of what has transpired.

## Job Offer Considerations

For many recent college graduates, the thrill of their first job and, for some, the most substantial regular income they have ever earned seems an excess of good fortune coming at once. To question that first income or to be critical in any way of the conditions of employment at the time of the initial offer seems like looking a gift horse in the mouth. It doesn't seem to occur to many new hires even to attempt to negotiate any aspect of their first job. And, as many employers who deal with entry-level jobs for recent college graduates will readily confirm, the reality is that there simply isn't much movement in salary available to these new college recruits. The entry-level hire generally does not have an employment track record on a professional level to provide any leverage for negotiation. Real negotiations on salary, benefits, retirement provisions, and so forth come to those with significant employment records at higher income levels.

Of course, the job offer is more than just money. It can be composed of geographic assignment, duties and responsibilities, training, benefits, health and medical insurance, educational assistance, car allowance or company vehicle, and a host of other items. All of this is generally detailed in the formal letter that presents the final job offer. In most cases this is a follow-up to a personal phone call from the employer representative who has been principally responsible for your hiring process.

That initial telephone offer is certainly binding as a verbal agreement, but most firms follow up with a detailed letter outlining the most significant parts of your employment contract. You may, of course, choose to respond immediately at the time of the telephone offer (which would be considered a binding oral contract), but you will also be required to formally answer the letter of offer with a letter of acceptance, restating the salient elements of the employer's description of your position, salary, and benefits. This ensures that both parties are clear on the terms and conditions of employment and remuneration and any other outstanding aspects of the job offer.

## Is This the Job You Want?

Most new employees will respond affirmatively in writing, glad to be in the position to accept employment. If you've worked hard to get the offer and the job market is tight, other offers may not be in sight, so you will say, "Yes, I accept!" What is important here is that the job offer you accept be one that does fit your particular needs, values, and interests as you've outlined them in your self-assessment process. Moreover, it should be a job that will not only use your skills and education but also challenge you to develop new skills and talents.

Jobs are sometimes accepted too hastily, for the wrong reasons, and without proper scrutiny by the applicant. For example, an individual might readily accept a sales job only to find the continual rejection by potential clients unendurable. An office worker might realize within weeks the constraints of a desk job and yearn for more activity. Employment is an important part of our lives. It is, for most of our adult lives, our most continuous productive activity. We want to make good choices based on the right criteria.

If you have a low tolerance for risk, a job based on commission will certainly be very anxiety-provoking. If being near your family is important, issues of relocation could present a decision crisis for you. If you're an adventurous person, a job with frequent travel would provide needed excitement and be very desirable. The importance of income, the need to continue your education, your personal health situation—all of these have an impact on whether the job you are considering will ultimately meet your needs. Unless you've spent some time understanding and thinking about these issues, it will be difficult to evaluate offers you do receive.

More important, if you make a decision that you cannot tolerate and feel you must leave that job, you will then have both unemployment and self-esteem issues to contend with. These will combine to make the next job search tough going, indeed. So make your acceptance a carefully considered decision.

## Negotiate Your Offer

It may be that there is some aspect of your job offer that is not particularly attractive to you. Perhaps there is no relocation allotment to help you move your possessions, and this presents some financial hardship for you. It may be that the health insurance is less than you had hoped. Your initial assignment may be different from what you expected, either in its location or in the duties and responsibilities that comprise it. Or it may simply be that the salary is less than you anticipated. Other considerations may be your official starting date of employment, vacation time, evening hours, dates of training programs or schools, and other concerns.

If you are considering not accepting the job because of some item or items in the job offer "package" that do not meet your needs, you should know that most employers emphatically wish that you would bring that issue to their attention. It may be that the employer can alter it to make the offer more agreeable for you. In some cases it cannot be changed. In any event the employer would generally like to have the opportunity to try to remedy a difficulty rather than risk losing a good potential employee over an issue that might have been resolved. After all, they have spent time and funds in securing your services, and they certainly deserve an opportunity to resolve any possible differences.

Honesty is the best approach in discussing any objections or uneasiness you might have over the employer's offer. Having received your formal offer in writing, contact your employer representative and indicate your particular dissatisfaction in a straightforward manner. For example, you might explain that while you are very interested in being employed by this organization, the salary (or any other benefit) is less than you have determined you require. State the terms you need, and listen to the response. You may be asked to put this in writing, or you may be asked to hold off until the firm can decide on a response. If you are dealing with a senior representative of the organization, one who has been involved in hiring for some time, you may get an immediate response or a solid indication of possible outcomes.

Perhaps the issue is one of relocation. Your initial assignment is in the Midwest, and because you had indicated a strong West Coast preference, you are surprised at the actual assignment. You might simply indicate that while you understand the need for the company to assign you based on its needs, you are disappointed and had hoped to be placed on the West Coast. You could inquire if that were still possible and, if not, would it be reasonable to expect a West Coast relocation in the future.

If your request is presented in a reasonable way, most employers will not see this as jeopardizing your offer. If they can agree to your proposal, they will. If not, they will simply tell you so, and you may choose to continue your candidacy with them or remove yourself from consideration. The choice will be up to you.

Some firms will adjust benefits within their parameters to meet the candidate's need if at all possible. If a candidate requires a relocation cost allowance, he or she may be asked to forgo tuition benefits for the first year to accomplish this adjustment. An increase in life insurance may be adjusted by some other benefit trade-off; perhaps a family dental plan is not needed. In these decisions you are called upon, sometimes under time pressure, to know how you value these issues and how important each is to you.

Many employers find they are more comfortable negotiating for candidates who have unique qualifications or who bring especially needed expertise to the organization. Employers hiring large numbers of entry-level college graduates may be far more reluctant to accommodate any changes in offer conditions. They are well supplied with candidates with similar education and experience so that if rejected by one candidate, they can draw new candidates from an ample labor pool.

## Compare Offers

The condition of the economy, the job seeker's academic major and particular geographic job market, and individual needs and demands for certain employment conditions may not provide more than one job offer at a time. Some job seekers may feel that no reasonable offer should go unaccepted for the simple fear there won't be another.

In a tough job market, or if the job you seek is not widely available, or when your job search goes on too long and becomes difficult to sustain financially and emotionally, it may be necessary to accept an inferior offer. The alternative is continued unemployment. Even here, when you feel you don't have a choice, you can at least understand that in accepting this particular offer, there may be limitations and conditions you don't appreciate. At the time of acceptance, there were no other alternatives, but you can begin to use that position to gain the experience and talent to move toward a more attractive position.

Sometimes, however, more than one offer is received, and the candidate has the luxury of choice. If the job seeker knows what he or she wants and has done the necessary self-assessment honestly and thoroughly, it may be clear that one of the offers conforms more closely to those expressed wants and needs.

However, if, as so often happens, the offers are similar in terms of conditions and salary, the question then becomes which organization might provide the necessary climate, opportunities, and advantages for your professional development and growth. This is the time when solid employer research and astute questioning during the interviews really pay off. How much did you learn about the employer through your own research and skillful questioning? When the interviewer asked during the interview "Do you have any questions?" did you ask the kinds of questions that would help resolve a choice between one organization and another? Just as an employer must decide among numerous applicants, so must the applicant learn to assess the potential employer. Both are partners in the job search.

## Reneging on an Offer

An especially disturbing occurrence for employers and career counseling professionals is when a job seeker formally (either orally or by written contract) accepts employment with one organization and later reneges on the agreement and goes with another employer.

There are all kinds of rationalizations offered for this unethical behavior. None of them satisfies. The sad irony is that what the job seeker is willing to do to the employer—make a promise and then break it—he or she would be outraged to have done to him- or herself: have the job offer pulled. It is a very bad way to begin a career. It suggests the individual has not taken the time to do the necessary self-assessment and self-awareness exercises to think and judge critically. The new offer taken may, in fact, be no better or worse than the one refused. You should be aware that there have been incidents of legal action following job candidates' reneging on an offer. This adds a very sour note to what should be a harmonious beginning of a lifelong adventure.

# PART TWO

# THE CAREER PATHS

# 5

# Introduction to the Career Paths

*"The promises of yesterday are the taxes of today."*
—William Lyon Mackenzie King

Which area of accounting is the best fit for you? Examine your skills, abilities, strengths, weaknesses, standards, priorities, goals, dreams, and hopes. Then ask yourself the following questions:

- Am I more attracted to public accounting, private accounting, government accounting, or accounting education?
- Do I want a forty-hour-per-week job, or do I not mind working longer hours—sometimes much longer hours?
- Do I want to travel?
- Do I like the idea of being my own boss?
- Do I enjoy working with a limited number of people or with a larger number of people?
- Am I good at communicating information to others?
- Do I like to be in charge, or do I prefer to have others in charge?
- Do I enjoy teaching?
- Do I have a specific area in accounting that particularly interests me?
- Do I prefer to work at home on my own or with others in an office setting?

Answering these questions will help you determine how you can best express yourself in accounting.

## In This Book

Although this book does not provide information about every career that would be possible for an accounting major, the chapters that follow offer a considerable amount of information about many careers in this field and describe four career paths:

1. Public accounting
2. Management accounting
3. Government accounting
4. Accounting education

Accounting is a wide field that provides many opportunities to those who are willing to prepare themselves and work hard to achieve success. Read on to learn more about which area of accounting appeals to you most, and then take the necessary steps to fulfill your dreams.

> *"Far and away the best prize that life offers is the
> chance to work hard at work worth doing."*
> —THEODORE ROOSEVELT

# 6

# Path I: Public Accounting

*"Every good citizen . . . should be willing to devote a brief time during some one day in the year, when necessary, to the making up of a listing of his income for taxes . . . to contribute to his Government, not the scriptural tithe, but a small percentage of his net profits."*
—Representative Cordell Hull (1913)

All around the world, accounting is an integral part of every business. Once considered one of the quieter occupations, it has undergone a dramatic renaissance. Taxation and auditing are areas of great importance. In addition, accountants work in areas such as management consulting, litigation support, the implementation and maintenance of accounting software systems, estate planning, and personal financial planning. For all who decide to enter it and put in the required amount of effort, the accounting profession offers a wide variety of opportunities.

---

**HELP WANTED: PUBLIC ACCOUNTANT**

Our company, one of Chicago's top twenty-five public accounting firms, has a team-oriented, client-focused environment encouraging creativity, initiative, and the free flow of ideas. Our diversified client base consists of highly successful, privately held companies in a variety of industries; nonprofit organizations; and individuals. An excellent opportunity exists for a bright, ambitious, entrepreneurial individual with good business sense. Strong theoretical background (with the ability to apply it), excellent computer skills, and outstanding interpersonal skills are necessary. A bachelor's degree in accounting, CPA credentials, and recent public accounting experience are required. Please send résumé.

# Definition of the Career Path

Public accountants provide services to outside clients to ensure those entities comply with mandates related to financial reporting, recordkeeping, and taxation. Additionally, public accountants advise businesses on ways to improve efficiency, security, and profitability.

## Public Accountant or Certified Public Accountant

Public accountants (PAs) and certified public accountants (CPAs), who either head their own businesses or work for accounting firms, provide a broad range of accounting, auditing, tax, and consulting services for their clients, which may be individuals, corporations, governments, or nonprofit organizations. All public accountants perform similar duties, but CPAs have additional credentials. (See "Training and Qualifications" later in this chapter.)

Within each field, accountants may choose from a number of specialties. For example, some public accountants concentrate on tax matters, such as preparing individual income tax returns or advising companies of the tax advantages and disadvantages of certain business decisions. Others concentrate on consulting and offer advice on matters such as employee health-care benefits and compensation; the design of companies' accounting and data-processing systems; and controls to safeguard assets. Some specialize in forensic accounting—investigating and interpreting white-collar crimes, such as securities fraud and embezzlement, bankruptcies, and other complex and possibly criminal financial transactions. Still others work primarily in auditing—examining a client's financial statements and reporting to investors and authorities that the statements have been prepared and reported correctly.

The widespread use of computers has reduced the time spent on number crunching and paperwork for accountants. Now, with the aid of software packages, accountants summarize transactions in standard formats for financial records or organize data in special formats for financial analysis. Personal and laptop computers enable accountants and auditors in all fields, even those who work independently, to work at clients' offices, which increases efficiency and accountability.

In an accounting firm, meetings are a fact of life for all staff members—meetings with other members of the firm and meetings with clients. Documentation is another fact of life, so it is important for accountants to have a good command of the English language and to be comfortable with writing. It's crucial that the results of the accountant's work and any required follow-up actions be clearly communicated to the client.

In a large accounting firm, the amount of interaction an accountant has with people is considerable. First, the number of people from the firm's own staff involved in any given project may be quite large. Second, the client may have a number of its people devoted to a project. Then multiply both of those numbers by the number of projects or clients an accountant may be working with at any one time.

Since public accountants are free of special interest in one business or client, they can make fair, unbiased judgments. Often a person or business relies solely on a public accountant for advice on money management. Public accountants also give families advice on money and taxes. They prepare estate, gift, inheritance, and income tax statements. Public accountants work with lawyers and insurance and trust experts. Together they set up or carry out estate plans and take care of other money matters.

A CPA who has been with a firm five to seven years often reaches a supervisory level. That person may spend a large part of his or her time doing just that—supervising. He or she is responsible for getting returns out the door, keeping clients and partners happy, seeing to it that the staff is satisfied and busy, and making sure that projects get done both correctly and on time.

## Possible Job Titles

Accountant
Auditor
Certified public accountant
Consultant
External auditor
Forensic accountant
Junior accountant
Management analyst
Partner
Public accountant
Senior accountant
Tax specialist

## Possible Employers

Accountants and auditors held about 1.1 million jobs in 2002. They worked throughout private industry and government, with 20 percent working for accounting, tax preparation, bookkeeping, and payroll services firms. Approximately 10 percent were self-employed.

Nearly every organization that has an income must have an accountant, either full- or part-time, to help keep track of money issues. Therefore, accountants may be employed by an individual, a company, a corporation, or a nonprofit organization.

Most accountants and auditors work in urban areas where public accounting firms and central or regional offices of businesses are concentrated. The following are the largest firms, called the "Big Four":

- Deloitte and Touche, 10 Westport Rd., P.O. Box 820, Wilton, CT 06897, deloitte.com
- Ernst & Young, 5 Times Square, New York, NY 10036, ey.com
- KPMG, 345 Park Ave., New York, NY 10154, kpmg.com
- PricewaterhouseCoopers, 1177 Avenue of the Americas, New York, NY 10036, pwc.com

## Related Occupations

Accountants and auditors analyze financial information and design internal control systems. Others for whom training in accounting is valuable include appraisers, cost estimators, bookkeeping clerks, those working in bank services, loan officers, financial analysts and personal financial advisors, bank officers, actuaries, underwriters, accounting and auditing clerks, securities sales representatives, bill and account collectors, and purchasing agents.

## Working Conditions

Accountants and auditors often work in offices, but public accountants may frequently visit the offices of clients while conducting audits, checking record-keeping, or preparing financial reports. Self-employed accountants may be able to do part of their work at home.

A large number of accountants and auditors generally work a standard forty-hour week, but many work longer, particularly if they are self-employed and free to take on the work of as many clients as they choose. Tax specialists often work long hours during the tax season—January through April 15.

The profession involves considerable contact with customers and the possibility of travel.

## Training and Qualifications

Those planning a career in accounting should have an aptitude for mathematics; be able to analyze, compare, and interpret facts and figures quickly and then make sound judgments based upon this knowledge; and have high standards of integrity, since financial decisions are made based on accountants' statements and services. Accountants must be able to clearly communicate the results of their work, both orally and in writing. Accountants and auditors also must be good at working with people, as well as with business systems and computers. Desirable personal traits include dedication, patience, integrity, and accuracy.

Most public accounting and business firms require applicants for accountant and auditor positions to have at least a bachelor's degree in accounting or a related field. Some employers prefer applicants with a master's degree in accounting or an M.B.A. with an accounting concentration. A multitude of four-year institutions offers accounting majors or minors. Private business schools, junior colleges, and some technical schools also offer training programs, but view these programs as the first step toward a minimum of a bachelor's degree if you want to be eligible for advancement in an accounting field.

Previous experience in accounting or auditing can help an applicant get a job. Many colleges offer students an opportunity to gain experience through summer or part-time internship programs conducted by public accounting or business firms. In addition, practical knowledge of computers and their applications in accounting is a great asset for job seekers in the accounting arena.

Professional recognition through certification or licensing provides a distinct advantage in the job market. Anyone working as a CPA is licensed by a state board of accountancy. The vast majority of states require CPA candidates to be college graduates, but a few states substitute a certain number of years of public accounting experience for the educational requirement. As of early 2003, based on recommendations made by the American Institute of Certified Public Accountants (AICPA), forty-two states and the District of Columbia require that CPA candidates complete 150 semester hours of college course work. This rule requires an additional 30 hours of course work beyond the usual four-year bachelor's degree, although the composition of these courses is unspecified by most states. Another five states have adopted similar legislation that will become effective by 2009. Many schools have altered their curricula so that they offer master's degrees as part of the 150 hours. Be sure to carefully research programs of study and state licensure requirements.

All states use the four-part Uniform CPA Examination prepared by the AICPA. The two-day CPA examination is rigorous, and only about one-quarter of those who take it each year pass each part they attempt. Candidates are not required to pass all four parts at once, although most states require candidates to pass at least two parts for partial credit and to successfully complete all sections of the test within a certain period of time. In 2004, the CPA exam became computerized and is offered quarterly at various testing sites throughout the United States. Most states require applicants for a CPA certificate to have some accounting experience in addition to having passed all parts of the exam.

The AICPA also offers members with valid CPA certificates the option to receive the Accredited in Business Valuation (ABV), Certified Information Technology Professional (CITP), or Personal Financial Specialist (PFS) designation. These designations distinguish those accountants with a certain level of expertise in the nontraditional areas in which accountants are practicing more frequently. The ABV designation requires a written exam and completion of a minimum of ten business valuation projects that demonstrate a candidate's experience and competence. The CITP requires payment of a fee, a written statement of intent, and the achievement of a set number of points awarded for business experience and education. Those who do not meet the required number of points may substitute a written exam. Candidates for the PFS designation also must achieve a certain level of points, based on experience and education, and they must pass a written exam and submit references.

Nearly all states require CPAs and other public accountants to complete a certain number of hours of continuing professional education before their licenses can be renewed. The professional associations representing accountants sponsor numerous courses, seminars, group study programs, and other forms of continuing education.

Professional societies bestow other forms of credentials on a voluntary basis. Voluntary certification can attest to professional competence in a specialized field of accounting and auditing. It also can certify that a recognized level of professional competence has been achieved by accountants and auditors who acquired some skills on the job, without the amount of formal education or public accounting work experience needed to meet the rigorous standards required to take the CPA examination.

Although continuing education may not be required for nonlicensed public accountants, all in the field will need to study industry publications to stay current.

## Earnings

According to a salary survey conducted by the National Association of Colleges and Employers, candidates with a bachelor's degree in accounting received starting offers averaging $40,647 a year in 2003; those with a master's degree in accounting, $42,241. In 2002, the median wage and annual salary earnings of accountants and auditors equaled $47,000. The middle half of the occupation earned between $37,210 and $61,630. The top 10 percent of accountants and auditors earned more than $82,730, and the bottom 10 percent earned less than $30,320.

Most full-time accounting professionals receive benefits that include paid vacations, health insurance, and pension plans. In smaller firms, the benefit offerings may be more limited than in larger firms.

## Career Outlook

Those who pursue CPA certification should have excellent job prospects, especially as more states enact the 150-hour requirement, making it more difficult to become a CPA. Competition for the most prestigious jobs, such as those with major accounting and business firms, will remain keen. Applicants with a master's degree in accounting or a master's degree in business administration with a concentration in accounting are increasingly valued, particularly among large firms. As computers now perform many increasingly complex accounting functions and allow accountants and auditors to analyze more information, a broad base of computer experience is also advantageous. Expertise in specialized areas, such as international business, computer systems, specific industries, or current legislation, may also be helpful in landing certain jobs.

Employment of accountants and auditors is expected to grow about as fast as the average for all occupations through the year 2012. In addition to openings resulting from growth, the need to replace accountants and auditors who retire or move into other fields will produce numerous job openings.

As the economy grows, the number of business establishments increases, requiring more accountants and auditors to set up books, prepare taxes, and provide management advice. This growth results in the increased volume and complexity of information developed by accountants and auditors on costs, expenditures, and taxes. Changes in legislation related to taxes, financial reporting standards, business investments, mergers, and other financial matters will create more jobs, too. The growth of international business has also led to more demand for accounting expertise and services related to international trade, accounting rules, mergers, and acquisitions. Increased awareness of financial crimes, such as bribery and securities fraud, will increase the demand for forensic accountants to detect illegal financial activity by individuals, companies, and organized crime rings. Computer technology has made these crimes easier to commit, and they are on the rise. But development of new computer software and electronic surveillance technology has also made tracking down financial criminals easier. As success rates of investigations grow, demand will also grow for forensic accountants.

The changing roles of public accountants and auditors also will spur job growth, although this growth will be limited as a result of financial scandals. In response to demand, in the past some accountants were offering more financial management and consulting services as they assumed a greater advisory role and developed more sophisticated accounting systems. Since federal legislation now prohibits accountants from providing nontraditional services to clients whose books they audit, opportunities for accountants to do nonaudit work could be limited. However, accountants will still be able to offer advice on other financial matters for clients that are not publicly traded companies as well as for nonaudit clients—but growth in these areas will be slower than in the past.

## Strategy for Finding the Jobs

A large number of accountants are hired into CPA firms directly out of school. Many of the larger firms recruit on college and graduate school campuses, or you can apply directly to a firm. Some job seekers consult with employment agents to learn of job openings. Typical sources of job ads— newspapers, industry publications, and the Internet—are other avenues to pursue.

Candidates who have managed to gain some basic accounting work experience during college and have served at least one internship have an edge in the hiring process. For today's accountant, there is growing emphasis on specializing, so you can also secure an advantage in the job market by studying an area of specialization.

## Public Accounting in Canada

Financial auditors in Canada examine and analyze financial records and check for compliance with proper accounting procedures. Accountants work with accounting systems to prepare individuals' and entities' financial information. Approximately four in ten financial auditors and accountants work in professional business services, either for a firm or through self-employment. Auditors and accountants with sufficient work experience are eligible to move into senior manager positions.

To become an accountant, you must usually complete a university degree and a professional accounting program, obtain on-the-job training, gain accreditation by a professional association, and be licensed in the geographic region of your employment. Financial auditors also have work experience as an accountant.

Designation as a chartered accountant (CA) recognizes that you adhere to high professional standards and have completed the rigorous requirements necessary to become a CA. These requirements include completing a professional training program that is approved by an institute of chartered accountants, twenty-four to thirty months of on-the-job training with a CA in a specially recognized training office, and successful completion of the three-day uniform evaluation. Through additional study, specialist designations are available to CAs. These specialties include investigative and forensic accounting, business valuation, insolvency and restructuring, and information technology.

Some accountants become certified general accountants (CGAs). CGAs are professional accountants who work in private practice or for the government. For the CGA certification, your professional training program must be one that is approved by the Society of Certified General Accountants. Before receiving CGA accreditation, you are evaluated on 147 competencies. The final requirement of CGA certification is the Professional Admission Comprehensive Examination.

According to the Department of Human Resources Development Canada, the average hourly wage for financial auditors and accountants is C$22.62. The Department also reports that the job outlook through the next several years is fair. One factor affecting this rating is the increased use of accounting software, which has reduced staffing needs. Generally, the number of people seeking employment in this field equals the number leaving jobs in the field. Alberta, British Columbia, and Ontario employ the highest numbers of auditors and accountants.

## Professional Associations

**American Institute of Certified Public Accountants (AICPA)**
1211 Avenue of the Americas
New York, NY 10036
aicpa.org

**American Society of Women Accountants (ASWA)**
8405 Greensboro Dr., Suite 800
McLean, VA 22102
aswa.org

**American Woman's Society of Certified Public**
 **Accountants (AWSCPA)**
136 S. Keowee St.
Dayton, OH 45402
awscpa.org

**The Canadian Institute of Chartered Accountants**
277 Wellington St. W
Toronto ON M5V 3H2
Canada
cica.ca

**CGA-Canada**
800-1188 W. Georgia St.
Vancouver, BC V6E 4A2
Canada
cga-canada.org

**The Information Systems Audit and Control**
 **Association (ISACA)**
3701 Algonquin Rd., Suite 1010
Rolling Meadows, IL 60008
isaca.org

**National Association of Forensic Accountants (NAFA)**
2455 East Sunrise Blvd., Suite 1201
Fort Lauderdale, FL 33304
nafanet.com

**National Association of State Boards of Accountancy (NASBA)**
150 Fourth Ave. N, Suite 700
Nashville, TN 37219
nasba.org

**National Society of Accountants (NSA)**
1010 N. Fairfax St.
Alexandria, VA 22314
nsacct.org

# Interviews with Professionals

The following interviews show how varied public accounting jobs can be.

### Meet Debra Schill

Debra Schill earned a bachelor of general studies degree from Indiana University in Indianapolis, majoring in business/accounting. She is a CPA with an Indiana license, a self-employed CPA in public accounting, and a financial planner. She also owns a Triple Check business, which includes Triple Check Income Tax Services, Triple Check Financial Services, and Triple Check Business Services.

"I was attracted to the profession because I really enjoyed preparing taxes," she says. "Since that work was seasonal, I decided that I would also enjoy doing similar work year-round, so I changed my college major from computer science to accounting. While in college, I worked for several years in the banking industry, first as a teller and then as a bookkeeper, proof operator, and clerk in the trust department. At the same time, I also worked part-time as a tax preparer for an H&R Block office.

"The tasks I enjoyed most in each of those jobs had to do with finances. I enjoyed handling money, was fascinated by the wealth I saw some individuals accumulate, and enjoyed watching how they managed it. I always liked doing data-entry work and filling out forms, and I had a good ability for solving problems. It seemed that by becoming an accountant and financial planner, I would be able to work with people in many areas, help them accumulate wealth, and manage that wealth through investment planning and wise tax planning.

"In September of 1994, I purchased an existing tax and bookkeeping business. The company's workload varies according to the time of the year. During tax season (January through April), I work seven days a week, from six to eighteen hours per day. The days are filled with appointments with clients to collect information for their tax returns. During tax season, evenings and weekends are dedicated to filling out those tax returns and getting them processed and out the door. During this time my office is hectic, with lots of people coming and going. During the rest of the year, my hours are usually from nine to five, with an occasional evening or weekend appointment. This is also a time when I concentrate on marketing plans to help my business grow and see clients for financial planning and tax planning, while managing the work schedules for two or more employees.

"I really enjoy working with people and helping them solve their financial problems. I can help them plan their financial futures and accomplish their goals. The downside for me would be the sales and marketing necessary to grow my business. I don't enjoy the sales responsibilities, which include cold-calling and making new contacts. I would rather have referrals of new business from my clients."

Debra's job situation exemplifies at least two of the commonly needed requirements of accountants: the need for excellent interpersonal skills and the ability to handle heavy workloads. Debra points out that with the demands of a job like hers, "You need to have a lot of support from your family." She adds, "Many spouses and children simply don't understand the commitment necessary, and it can cause problems."

## Meet Gerri Green

Gerri Green earned a bachelor's degree in psychology at the University of Connecticut and her M.B.A. in accounting at the University of Hartford. She now serves as a CPA in the state of Connecticut. During her twenty-two years in the accounting field, she has been employed by a very small local CPA firm as a staff accountant, a huge insurance company, a Big Six CPA firm as a tax supervisor, a Fortune 500 corporation as a U.S. tax manager, a medium-sized CPA firm, a family-owned business as a consultant, and a medium-sized CPA firm as a partner (first part-time, then full-time).

She is also a part-time freelance writer who has received the Distinguished Author Award from the Connecticut Society of CPAs and has served as editor of an accounting journal and chair of the Connecticut Society of CPAs' publications committee.

"For the past eight years, I have also served as an adjunct accounting teacher and adviser for students at the college level," she says. "Several years ago, I seriously explored the possibility of getting my Ph.D. in accounting so I could teach full-time, research, and write. The first year I applied, I was on the waiting list. The second year, I could have gone, but I made partner at the CPA firm I was with, so I decided against school.

"Several months ago, I left my position as partner of a CPA firm. I had joined that firm four years ago (after thoughtful reflection on all my other experiences) to work in a small-firm environment. It was wonderful until early this year, when the firm merged with two others to form the largest non–Big Six firm in the area. Since this change included a move into an office tower in the city, I made the decision to leave. My already long commute would have been even longer, and I wanted more flexibility with my time and my life than the new firm would have provided. Now I'm engaged in Internet training for CPAs and others and doing more writing. And I look forward to whatever is next!"

## Meet Liane Michele Lemons

Liane Michele Lemons is a graduate of Boise State University in Boise, Idaho, having received her bachelor of arts degree in accounting. Presently, she is the owner of her own tax practice in Boise.

"My first accounting job was in 1986 as an accounting intern for the Internal Revenue Service," she says. "After graduating in 1987, I became a revenue agent (auditor) for the IRS.

"Since I am a small-business owner who focuses on small businesses, my work atmosphere is very casual. We don't frequently dress up or even have a strict dress code. The work is very hectic. A typical day would include bookkeeping, speaking with the IRS, preparing reports, doing taxes, and meeting with clients. No two days are ever the same, nor are any two clients. I take a personal interest in my clients, so I have the opportunity to meet many interesting people.

"I typically work forty to fifty hours a week during the off season, and from 9 A.M. until midnight during tax season. Demands change on a daily basis, and stress is very high for me on most days. I spend a lot of time responding to problems and putting out fires. I find that I have to take time off to keep from burning out. I spend almost all day in front of a computer and have become a lot more computer literate than I ever imagined I would be. Since I engage in both tax work and accounting, I constantly face looming deadlines, which adds to the pressure of the day. However, I do enjoy my work and feel I am very good at it. In fact, I was named the Region X

Accountant Advocate of the Year by the United States Small Business Administration.

"I am happy that I have the ability to meet and observe a variety of people in vastly different economic and social circumstances. I also get to know and understand a lot of different businesses and industries intimately, which is very rewarding both to me and my clients. I truly enjoy seeing the work I do help people succeed. The thing that I like least is having to be at my clients' beck and call. Some people act as if they are the only client I have, and they expect to be given top priority every time they call. It is also frustrating to deal with people who don't listen and then end up in trouble as a result of ignoring my advice."

In accounting, you often have to start at a very basic level to gain the experience needed for the growth opportunities that exist. This was true with Liane, who was once an intern and is now a business owner. Your early days as an accountant usually require day-to-day detail and repetition, but these help build the foundation on which you can build whatever career path you desire.

## Meet Thomas R. Hileman

Thomas R. Hileman received his bachelor of science degree from Penn State University in 1972. He now serves as president/shareholder of Hileman and Associates, PC.

"I started in accounting in 1972 after graduation," he says. "In 1973, I began to do public accounting and realized I loved it. No two problems were the same, and I got to work with a lot of people. Since I am a people person, that was a plus. I struck out on my own in 1983 and have never looked back. I was attracted to the freedoms it provided for me. If you are successful in public accounting, you can pick and choose your clients. I am very happy to say that most of my clients are now good friends.

"Because of the nature of my practice, I spend a large portion of my day on the phone with clients trying to solve their problems. If the client is big enough, they might have someone on staff to handle some of what I do, although one of my clients is a $40-million-a-year concern and I function almost as its chief financial officer (CFO). No major financial decisions are made without my involvement.

"My office has a friendly, almost homey atmosphere. Because we have to put in long hours on various special projects such as litigation support, we are pretty laid back most of the time. In fact, on Fridays everyone can dress in business casual.

"I really enjoy the people, the mental challenges, and the fact that I am financially rewarded for my efforts. What I like least are the hours and having to always be in the client acquisition mode."

Thomas advises those interested in public accounting to work for a firm with good technical capabilities. He also recommends that you work in as many areas as possible. Don't limit yourself to just tax work or audit work. The varied work experience will provide a good background on which to draw.

## Meet Sherry L. McCoy

Sherry L. McCoy earned dual bachelor of science degrees in business from Eastern Illinois University—one in accounting and one in finance. Landing a position with McGladrey and Pullen, LLP, in Peoria, Illinois, in June 1990 through campus recruiting, she now serves as general services manager for her company's branch office in Pasadena, California.

"During my freshman or sophomore year in high school," she says, "I did a career research paper on accounting, learning that in England, CPAs are called 'chartered accountants.' The rest, as they say, is history. My first (and only) accounting class in high school was the perfect preparation for college. The teacher and I bonded. Without a doubt, that course was the foundation for my perfect test scores in my first college accounting course!

"I could mention many professors and administrators at Eastern Illinois University, throughout the business department and other disciplines, who played a key role in those formative years. However, for brevity, I will simply say that we are all a product of our past, and I am deeply thankful for those whose paths I crossed. And to my parents, who never put barriers on my own testing and stretching of abilities, eternal thanks!

"My degrees are in accounting and finance, and while I was relatively certain of accounting as a career, I had an interest in finance courses due to the practical nature of information such as banking, insurance, real estate—all are things we need for daily living from a financial perspective.

"I did work for Ford Motor Credit Company during two summers of my college career. The staff there was great, but I knew I didn't want to spend the first few years of my professional career making credit collection calls. So I focused on accounting, particularly public accounting, since it seemed to offer the greatest exposure to a variety of people and industries.

"Like the saying goes, the only constant in change is constant change. So it is with my days. Of course, there is always a general scheme of events, but many days are spent simply being flexible when it comes to specifics. Likewise, some days are unbelievably busy while others proceed at a much more manageable rate (and on most days, I don't know which will occur).

"I wish I could outline a typical day—but there's really no such thing, in my opinion, unless you want to be extremely general in the discussion. In that case, most days begin with a cup of coffee and a review of the day's calendar while checking voice mail and e-mail for new messages. From there, days are spent in the office or at a client location (with many days including a bit of both). My present responsibilities basically focus on client service in the area of financial and compliance auditing, with general business advice also included, and staff training. The public accounting industry is heavily reliant on on-the-job training. Thus, in most cases, I fulfill both of these responsibilities concurrently. In an environment where efficiency is highly regarded, this is especially important and rewarding as well."

Sherry's typical schedule is similar to that of many other accountants: her work is heaviest from October to March, especially January to March, when financial statements are prepared and tax-related activities are performed. After April 15, a forty-hour workweek is typical.

Sherry comments, "I have been fortunate to have excellent colleagues in the firm—both advisers and advisees. A variety of individuals have taken time to train me, and I certainly do my best to do the same, which is easy when you have a staff of people who are willing and able to learn and grow. Similarly, working with clients, no matter what the role, has been both challenging and rewarding, just more proof that life is really all about people!

"What I like most about public accounting at McGladrey and Pullen, LLP, is the variety: people, industries, job details, new ideas. I really can't imagine another job in which I could have the same variety of experiences, from walking into bank vaults for surprise cash counts to being fork-lifted to count Jacuzzis in a home improvement warehouse.

"The downside can sometimes also be variety—too many different directions to go in and only one of me to get everything done. But the upside definitely surpasses those moments. If it weren't so, I would not continue in this line of work."

Anyone contemplating an accounting field needs to be prepared for the quick changes that can occur in one's priority list. Each new day can be different from the last and may not be what you expect it to be.

## Meet M. L. Josette Hewitt

M. L. Josette Hewitt earned a bachelor of science degree in commerce with a major in accounting, graduating cum laude. She has a diploma in industrial relations and is a certified financial planner with security licenses in life, fire and casualty, disability, and health insurance. She is an enrolled agent, certified financial planner, registered representative, insurance broker, and business consultant. After spending ten years as a CPA in the Philippines, she came to the United States and began working as a tax preparer. In 1990, she became a Triple Check Income Tax Services licensee. Recently she branched out from the traditional accounting/tax consulting business to become a licensee of both Triple Check Financial Services and Triple Check Business Services as well.

"I had a desire to assist individuals and small-business owners in organizing their tax, bookkeeping, and financial status," she says. "Other than during income tax season, we have a very flexible time schedule to meet with our clients in a relaxed and comfortable manner. I like clients who are organized and up-to-date and who provide us with complete and current records and documents. I also appreciate those who realize the hard work that we do. I dislike clients who want us to do a lot of work but do not have the finances to pay our fees.

"I would advise others who are interested in this field to always be aggressive and to maintain a good attitude toward people."

### Meet Frederick R. Berk

Frederick R. Berk received his bachelor of science degree in accounting from the State University of New York at Binghamton and obtained his CPA license in 1984. He is a partner at Friedman, Alpren and Green, LLP, where he serves in the real estate group. With extensive knowledge in real estate taxation, accounting, and auditing, he has participated in construction and development activities, income taxation, restructuring, and consulting. Recently, he has become involved with consulting and tax planning regarding passive losses, cancellation of indebtedness, real estate professional regulations, and the formation of real estate investment trusts. In addition, he represents numerous institutions in loan restructuring and property cash flow analysis, which is utilized to determine the money due to the institutions. He has also authored several real estate articles and is a member of the American Institute of Certified Public Accountants, the New York State Society of Certified Public Accounts (where he serves as a member of the real estate committee), and the National Realty Club. He is also treasurer of the Young Mortgage Bankers Association.

"I took an accounting course in high school, which I enjoyed," he says. "I was intrigued with the fact that someone could become a partner in an accounting firm with eight to twelve years of experience. I worked on numerous jobs while in high school and college and decided that this profession would provide me with a desirable path to success.

"I started in the accounting field in 1981 after college graduation. Though I received job offers from the Big Six, I decided that I would rather work for a smaller firm. At the time, Friedman, Alpren and Green, LLP, employed approximately 40 people. (Today we work with 115 people.)

"In a service business with numerous clients (or, as I refer to them, my bosses) all demanding expedient high-quality service, the day is extremely busy and sometimes hectic. Work hours vary from thirty-five to seventy-five hours per week. It is an atmosphere where people are professional and courteous.

"I enjoy working with numerous clients," he adds, "and being involved in several different engagements at a time. I also enjoy interacting with our staff. However, I would like to be able to spend more time with my family."

Frederick confirms the need for skills beyond accounting knowledge, specifically technical proficiency and the ability to establish good working relationships—with clients and with other accounting professionals.

## Meet John R. Baker

John R. Baker earned a bachelor of science degree in accounting from Rockhurst College in Kansas City, Missouri. He is president of Troupe, Kehoe, Whiteaker & Kent, LLC, in Kansas City, Missouri; a licensed CPA in the states of Missouri and Kansas; and a member of the Missouri Society of Certified Public Accountants and the American Institute of Certified Public Accountants.

"Accounting has interested me since I was in high school," he says. "So when I entered college I made it my major. Over the years, I have grown with the practice. (This firm is a third-generation firm.) Also, over the years I have worked my way up from junior accountant, to junior auditor, to individual in charge of audits, to manager, to partner.

"The work atmosphere is pretty relaxed. We are family-oriented, with plenty of flexibility. Everyone is a professional, so each person does what it takes to get the job done. We maintain an open-door policy and are here to listen to our employees. Because of this, there isn't a division among staff. We expect everyone to do a quality job and get the job done.

"I like the people contact best, particularly the one-to-one time spent with clients. Anyone can crunch numbers or be technically competent, but working with people makes this job interesting. I least like having to account for every quarter-hour of my time.

"There is no typical day. I usually arrive at the office at 7:45 A.M. and leave around 6:00 P.M., putting in about fifty-five to sixty hours per week. I have a certain number of appointments, but things are constantly changing. It's like a moving target all the time. On average, 35 percent of my time is spent on administration and about 25 percent reviewing the work of other staff members. The remainder of my time is spent on daily duties, management issues, and special projects for clients. Our busiest season is January through April, and summer can also be quite strenuous."

John attributes an accountant's success to, among other things, flexibility, good communication skills, good interpersonal skills, high-quality accounting skills, good marketing skills, effective networking, and excellent computer skills.

## Meet Stuart Kessler

Stuart Kessler earned a bachelor of arts degree from Brooklyn College, an M.B.A. from City College of New York, a Juris Doctor from Brooklyn Law School, and a master of laws (L.L.M.) degree in taxation from New York University. He has earned the Personal Financial Planning Specialist designation, was elected chair of the American Institute of Certified Public Accountants, and is past president of the New York State Society of Certified Public Accountants. He is now a partner in the accounting firm of Goldstein, Golub, and Kessler.

"Accounting is a people-oriented profession," he says. "To me, the prospect of joining the accounting profession was attractive because of the ease of going from client to client and to different offices. I liked the idea of being in a position to meet new people all the time.

"An average day includes a large number of meetings, phone calls, e-mails, and voice mails. The communications technology is very different now than it was when I began in this profession," he stresses.

"I meet with a number of clients every day on personal financial planning and tax issues," he says. "Some meetings are prospect or client lunches and there are also evening professional and social activities like tennis. Also, a considerable amount of time is spent in fulfilling professional obligations, such as for the AICPA.

"The atmosphere is professional, friendly, diligent, and conducive to learning. The hours can be long when you have many meetings and client appointments out of the office on a given day.

"What I enjoy most is the personal aspect of the job—dealing with clients and their families. I enjoy meeting and working with a lot of good people, many of whom I have made long-term friends (some for thirty to forty-five years). To some degree, a CPA is closer to her clients than any other professional, including a psychiatrist.

"What I like least are internal meetings (not involving clients), and billing and collection. It's also quite a challenge to keep up with the constant changes in law, especially tax law. There is a constant need to be on the leading edge, which requires a lot of outside reading.

"I would advise those interested in this field to take as many courses in liberal arts as possible, specifically writing, speech rhetoric, and reading comprehension."

### Meet Susan Wilt

Susan Wilt earned a bachelor of science degree in accounting from the University of Kansas in Lawrence, Kansas. She is presently employed by Arthur Andersen in Kansas City, Missouri, as a financial analyst.

"I have a strong math aptitude and knew I wanted to be an accountant after my first accounting class in college," she says. "I began working for Arthur Andersen right out of college.

"I enjoy the problem solving. Resolution is very rewarding to me. However, there is never a day that you really feel as if you are done. And the competition is perpetual."

Susan's typical workweek is fifty hours, more than the average number of hours for accountants. Her work duties, however, are typical for today's accountant—lots of paperwork, analysis, and customer service. These sample duties are indicative of why an accountant should love working with numbers and compiling various reports—jobs that can make long days seem longer if you don't love what you're doing.

### Meet Alan P. Sklar

In 1960, Alan P. Sklar earned a bachelor of science and bachelor of arts (B.S.B.A.) degree from Northwestern University, Evanston, Illinois. He is a licensed CPA in Illinois and a senior partner with Gleeson, Sklar, Sawyers, and Cumpata, LLP, in Skokie, Illinois. He has had experience with both a national and a local CPA firm.

"I liked math and thought that accounting was all math," he says. "I was wrong about that but I still ventured into the right profession.

"I founded this firm in 1967 (upon leaving the firm I was at after being offered a partnership) because I thought I could be more successful and have more control over the future on my own. Because we brought bright people into the firm, we now are a second-generation firm with more than eighty people.

"My job is made up of three major areas: managing people and jobs; acting as a consultant in many areas; and business development. A typical day might include breakfast, lunch, or even golf with contacts (brokers or lawyers) or clients. It could include conferences with the managers regarding the status of client engagements. It also could include telephone conferences or face-to-face meetings and consulting with clients.

"I like working with clients the most. It's very rewarding when you have helped a client's business."

Although Alan pursued a career in accounting because he loved math, he has learned that accounting is much more than working with numbers. It also requires writing and interpersonal skills. Additionally, Alan recommends that early on an accountant develop a specific consulting skill through education beyond a bachelor's degree.

## Meet George Simpson

George Simpson earned a bachelor of science degree with an accounting emphasis from California State University at Los Angeles in 1965. He received his California CPA certificate in 1973 and his financial planning specialist designation from the AICPA in 1992. He is chief executive officer of a large tax preparation, financial service, and business service office located in southern California.

"I started preparing taxes in 1969 while working at Lockheed Aircraft. When one of my coworkers who prepared taxes part-time became ill, he asked me to help him out. In 1971, I started working for a CPA doing taxes full-time and have been preparing taxes ever since.

"I love the challenge tax preparation offers. I enjoy helping others achieve their goals and prepare for their futures. I love to be creative in the interpretation of the tax laws.

"I was the accountant for my father's business while in high school and college. I then worked in the financial arena prior to working for the CPA in 1971.

"My job is stressful. I have eight employees that I have to challenge and direct. I have more than 1,200 personal tax clients, plus an additional 1,400 in the office. During tax season I work from 8 A.M. to 11 P.M. Monday to Friday, 8 A.M. until 6 P.M. on Saturday, and noon to 6 P.M. on Sunday every week. The remaining weeks I work from 8 A.M. until 6 P.M. Monday to Friday. I spend my days preparing taxes, providing financial advice, and being available to staff. The atmosphere is congenial and enjoyable."

Work schedules such as George's show why accounting professionals need a good work ethic and a positive attitude. His job also portrays an accounting field that has changed over time to involve more sales work and an increased level of involvement with people outside the firm. Even with all the demands, George says, "There is very little I can say that is negative. Employee problems are sometimes stressful and tax season has many hours without a break, but it is what I live for. I've never regretted what I do for a living for a single day."

# 7

# Path 2: Management Accounting

*"Taxes, after all, are the dues that we pay for the*
*privileges of membership in an organized society."*
—Franklin D. Roosevelt

Management accountants compose the largest group of accounting professionals. They are employed by industry or business firms to provide advice and make decisions related to financial investment, budgeting, forecasting, and other business operations. Frequently, they work under the direction of corporate controllers and, in turn, supervise a staff of accounting personnel.

## HELP WANTED: ACCOUNTANT

The world's largest trading center for limited-edition collector's bells and one of the most successful marketers of collectible items is seeking accounting professionals to join our team. You'll work in our financial area, which handles the corporate accounting functions as well as financial analysis and reporting. You will be responsible for accounting, financial control and financial reporting, and analysis for a business unit. This position will focus on working with the marketing team to analyze activity as well as handle cash management. The qualified applicant must possess a B.A., accounting preferred, as well as a minimum of two years' experience with financial statement preparation and analysis. Computer proficiency is a must and previous mainframe responsibility a plus. We're looking for a self-starter with good communication skills who can effectively manage multiple priorities simultaneously. We offer a competitive salary and comprehensive benefits package. Please forward your résumé and salary history to us.

## Definition of the Career Path

Management accountants are also often called cost, managerial, industrial, corporate, or private accountants. In their capacity as accounting professionals, they record and analyze the financial information of the companies for which they work. They also are responsible for budgeting, performance evaluation, cost management, and asset management. They are usually part of executive teams that are involved in strategic planning or new product development.

Management accountants analyze and interpret the financial information corporate executives need to make sound business decisions. They also prepare financial reports for nonmanagement groups, including stockholders, creditors, regulatory agencies, and tax authorities. Within accounting departments, they work in various areas that include financial analysis, planning and budgeting, and cost accounting.

From the start, management accountants must demonstrate their basic accounting techniques and ability to handle assignments. Mastering the various functions of their departments and understanding how their departments fit in the accounting structure are vital. At first, preparing reports and other work will be done under the eyes of senior accountants. As one gains experience, additional responsibilities are added. At the entry level, typical tasks are in the areas of receivables, payables, payroll, and general ledger. After establishing competence, more advanced projects, such as offering ideas on and testing improved accounting procedures, supervising general accounting work, and preparing reports on company finances, will be assigned.

Beginning management accountants often start as cost accountants, junior internal auditors, or trainees for other accounting positions. As they rise through the organization, they may advance to accounting manager, chief cost accountant, budget director, or manager of internal auditing. Some become controllers, treasurers, financial vice presidents, chief financial officers (CFOs), or corporation presidents. Many senior corporation executives have backgrounds in accounting, internal auditing, or finance.

A company's general accounting department handles daily business needs, such as maintaining accounting records, budgeting, balancing the books, and preparing financial statements. Accountants must pay close attention to all laws and regulations affecting daily business operations. In smaller firms, the general accountant might be the individual who handles or directs most or all accounting functions. In turn, this individual would work most closely with public accountants if the organization employs them.

In certain instances, businesses employ public accountants to conduct audits. In other situations, organizations divide their accounting needs between public and management accountants, giving some functions (such as taxes) to an outside firm and assigning day-to-day jobs (such as payroll and budgeting) to the internal staff. For this reason, the career paths and duties of management accountants vary considerably.

The following are some of the specialties followed by professionals in this field.

## Management Consultant

Management consultants work in cost accounting, planning and budgeting, financial analysis, and other activities They take part in problem-solving and decision-making processes in business. The work varies from job to job. They may help establish inventory controls, assist with corporate restructuring, or provide staffing for a special project. Management consultants need to be knowledgeable in a broad range of topics, including operations, finance, data processing, and general management.

## Tax Accountant

Tax accountants specialize in preparing and filing federal, state, and local tax returns and must be extremely knowledgeable about federal, state, and local tax laws. They examine accounts, records, and computer tax returns according to government regulations. They also may originate, revise, and install tax record systems, conduct research to determine the effects of taxes pertaining to business operations or decisions, and recommend alternate methods of operations to reduce tax liabilities.

## Cost Accountant

Cost accountants determine the cost of operating a firm or producing a product. They are responsible for identifying cost control procedures, supervising cost systems and methods, and compiling periodic reports of operating costs. Working with marketing and manufacturing departments, they devise computerized cost analyses of labor, materials, and overhead, which are involved in determining operating budgets, prices of products, profits, contract adjustments, and development of new products. Their expertise is needed by manufacturing and service industries alike.

## Budget Accountant

Budget accountants prepare budgets showing past and projected operating expenses, income, and profits; analyze the availability and effect of spending funds for capital investments (plant, equipment, and long-term product expenditures) and other major expenditures; and use budgeting systems to control various categories of expenditures. They prepare reports of

**HELP WANTED: STAFF ACCOUNTANT**

Downtown firm seeks individual for general accounting responsibilities. Successful candidate will be an energetic self-starter with a B.A. in accounting, computer skills, and analytical skills who learns quickly and works independently. Primary duties include accounts payable, accounts receivable, journal entries, bank reconciliations, and account analysis. This service firm has a growing residential real estate portfolio of apartment buildings. Salary in low- to midthirties. Forward résumé with salary history.

their findings, which are used as a basis for management planning and decisions.

## Systems Accountant

Systems accountants design, install, and review accounting systems and procedures. They determine which records and reports are necessary, examine current accounting methods, develop procedures for obtaining the needed information, and implement accounting systems that will accomplish the desired objectives. Systems accountants must be knowledgeable about data-processing methods and capable of operating such systems.

## Internal Auditor

Internal auditing is an increasingly important area of accounting and auditing. Internal auditors verify the accuracy of their organizations' internal records and check for mismanagement, waste, or fraud. They also examine and evaluate their firms' financial and information systems, management procedures, and internal controls to ensure that records are accurate and controls are adequate to protect against fraud and waste, and they review company operations to evaluate their efficiency, effectiveness, and compliance with corporate policies, laws, and government regulations. Many internal auditors become highly specialized in areas that include electronic data processing, engineering, insurance premiums, banking, and health care. As computer systems make information timelier, internal auditors help managers to base their decisions on actual data, rather than personal observation. Internal auditors also may recommend controls for their organizations' computer systems to ensure system reliability and data integrity.

In addition to being a skilled accountant, the internal auditor must have a comprehensive understanding of all fundamental business areas and the corporation's objectives. The internal auditor must be thoroughly knowledgeable about computer systems and the potential risks emerging in our electronic world. To do this type of work, one must be an individual of exceptional diligence and concentration.

Internal auditors may recommend controls for their organizations' computer systems to ensure the reliability of the systems and the integrity of the data. A growing number of accountants and auditors have extensive computer skills and specialize in correcting problems with software or developing software to meet unique data needs.

Internal auditors conduct operational audits, regulatory reviews, and other special projects. They look into operations such as research and development, production, personnel, marketing, and information systems. They recommend methods to increase efficiency, effectiveness, and profits.

In conducting an audit, internal auditors follow generally accepted auditing standards. They use sampling techniques to test the accuracy of transactions, the accounting system, and management information systems. They test the recorded amounts of inventories, property, and equipment. They compare orders and receipts with company records to confirm that transactions actually took place.

Internal auditors check inventories and audit payrolls. They look to see whether storage methods prevent theft or spoilage. Auditors may suggest a way to save energy and at the same time use by-products. They see whether the firm is meeting its schedules. They may make suggestions to reduce employee turnover. They are also alert to the possibilities of fraud or theft.

## HELP WANTED: SENIOR STAFF ACCOUNTANT

We are a premier manufacturer of quality office products. We seek a detail-oriented professional for our fast-paced finance department. The selected candidate will be responsible for the preparation and communication of consolidated financial statements, consolidated annual budget, and periodic consolidation forecasts. In addition, he will be involved with corporate LAN administration. This individual will be a degreed accountant with three years of experience, preferably in a manufacturing operating environment, who possesses the ability to communicate effectively. Computer proficiency a must. Public accounting background and CPA preferred. Business planning experience desired. We offer an excellent salary and benefits. Send résumé with salary history.

Reviewing and reporting to management about taxes, sales, purchasing, and advertising, internal auditors challenge the value of accounts receivable and look for unrecorded accounts payable. They are always looking for ways to improve productivity and cut costs.

## Controller

The controller is the executive in charge of all accounting functions and summarized financial information for executive personnel. The controller establishes finance-related policies and must have a keen understanding of all business operations and the judgment to make sound financial planning decisions.

## Treasurer

The treasurer handles the cash flow and all financial reserves and is involved with loans, credit, and investments. Some firms may combine the functions of controller and treasurer into one position.

## Chief Financial Officer

The CFO oversees the controller and treasurer and may oversee the chief internal auditor. The CFO advises top executives as to the financial needs and stability of the organization.

# Possible Job Titles

Accountant
Accounting manager
Auditor
Budget accountant
Budget director
Certified management accountant
Certified public accountant
Chief cost accountant
Chief financial officer
Chief internal auditor
Controller
Corporate accountant
Corporation president
Cost accountant
Financial vice president

General accountant
Industrial accountant
Internal auditor
Junior internal auditor
Management accountant
Management consultant
Managerial accountant
Manager of accounting
Manager of internal auditing
Private accountant
Property accountant
Senior accountant
Staff accountant
Systems accountant
Tax accountant
Treasurer

## Possible Employers

Management accountants may be hired by private businesses, nonprofit organizations, or industries, and they may find work in any part of the United States. Most are employed in urban areas where accounting firms and the headquarters of businesses are located.

### HELP WANTED: SENIOR ACCOUNTANT

The selected candidate will develop monthly, quarterly, and annual financial reports; assist with the preparation and analysis of statutory reporting requirements; audit the flow of statistical data from source documents through input to resultant output; write and update data retrieval programs; and write comprehensive status reports. The position requires strong deadline/time management and teamwork abilities. A B.S./B.A. in accounting or finance, more than three years' experience in accounting or finance, and experience with Excel, Word, and/or Access are essential. Insurance experience and/or a CPA a plus. Applicants must be able to work extra hours as needed.

---

**HELP WANTED: ACCOUNTANT**
_____

One of the largest real estate service companies in the world has an immediate
opportunity at our fast-paced Chicago Loop office. Candidate will be
responsible for preparing and reviewing monthly financial reporting packages,
forecasting, budgeting, monitoring cash flow, coordinating accounts payable, and
interfacing with clients. A bachelor's degree in accounting, one to two years of
related experience, and Excel proficiency required. Strong analytical skills and
the ability to work independently are essential. Please send résumé.

---

# Related Occupations

The Employment and Training Administration of the U.S. Department of
Labor classified accountants with workers in finance occupations that include
bursars, auditors, credit analysts, accounting methods analysts, accounting systems analysts, accounting technicians, bank examiners, financial advisors,
financial analysts, cost expeditors, production cost estimators, tax adjusters,
tax examiners, and tax experts.

# Working Conditions

Management accountants have either their own offices within a company or
cubicles or areas in which they operate. They use computers and other necessary office equipment. Since management accountants are employed by private business or industry, they are more apt to work a standard forty-hour
week than are public accountants.

# Training and Qualifications

High school students planning on embarking on an accounting career should
take courses to prepare for college, which include mathematics, science,
foreign language, public speaking, communications, English, and computer
technology.

Most private businesses hire only college graduates. Students should plan
to earn a minimum of a bachelor's degree. (Many firms prefer those with a
master's degree.) The major should be in accounting or in business admin-

istration with a minor in accounting. Students planning on an accounting career should look carefully at college programs before enrolling.

The Institute of Management Accountants (IMA) confers the certified management accountant (CMA) designation upon college graduates or applicants who attain a minimum score on specified graduate school entrance exams. Candidates for this certification must also pass a four-part examination, agree to meet continuing education requirements, comply with standards of professional conduct, and have at least two years' work experience in management accounting. The CMA program is administered through the Institute of Certified Management Accountants, an affiliate of the IMA.

The Institute of Internal Auditors (IIA) grants the designation certified internal auditor (CIA) to graduates of accredited colleges and universities who have had two years of experience in internal auditing and have passed a four-part examination. The IIA recently implemented three new specialty designations—certification in control self-assessment (CCSA), certified government auditing professional (CGAP), and certified financial services auditor (CFSA). Requirements are similar to those of the CIA.

The Information Systems Audit and Control Association grants the designation certified information systems auditor (CISA) to candidates who pass an examination and have five years of experience in auditing information systems. Auditing or data-processing experience and a college education may be substituted for up to two years of work experience.

Three of the designations conferred by the Accreditation Council for Accountancy and Taxation, a satellite organization of the National Society of Accountants, are accredited business accountant (ABA), accredited tax advisor (ATA), and accredited tax preparer (ATP). These accreditations are made on accountants specializing in tax preparation for small- and medium-sized businesses. Candidates for the ABA must pass an exam, while candidates for the ATA and ATP must complete the required course work *and* pass an exam.

Multiple certification is common and encouraged. For instance, an internal auditor might be a CPA, CIA, and CISA.

### HELP WANTED: STAFF ACCOUNTANT

Fast-paced, multidimensional accounting department seeks self-motivated, detail-oriented individual to perform variety of functions utilizing in-house computer accounting system, accounting analysis, and reconciliation. B.A. in accounting plus minimum of two years' experience required.

**HELP WANTED: ACCOUNTING—ENTRY LEVEL**

Our office seeks an accounting graduate for an entry-level position. Responsibilities include all aspects of financial statement preparation. Experience is not required, but willingness to learn, be part of our team, and get excited are. New grads welcome to apply.

In terms of personal abilities, accountants should be able to analyze, compare, and interpret facts and figures. They should have the ability to make sound judgments from this knowledge and be efficient problem solvers. Accountants should be able to concentrate for extended periods and be able communicators. Other qualities include reliability, accuracy, independence, personal responsibility, flexibility, and self-discipline. Accountants must work well with both people and business systems.

Computers are rapidly changing the nature of the work for most accountants and auditors. Accounting software packages greatly reduce the amount of tedious manual work associated with data management and recordkeeping. Computers enable accountants and auditors to be more mobile and to use their clients' computer systems to extract information from databases and the Internet. As a result, a growing number of accountants and auditors with extensive computer skills specialize in correcting problems with software or in developing software to meet unique data-management and analytical needs. Accountants also are beginning to perform more technical duties, such as implementing, controlling, and auditing systems and networks, and developing technology plans and budgets.

## Earnings

According to a 2004 survey by the National Association of Colleges and Employers, offers to graduates with a bachelor's degree in accounting averaged about $41,110. According to a 2003 salary survey conducted by Robert Half International, a staffing services firm specializing in accounting and finance, accountants and auditors with up to one year of experience earned between $29,500 and $40,500. Those with one to three years of experience earned between $34,000 and $49,500. Senior accountants and auditors earned between $41,000 and $61,500; managers earned between $47,500 and $78,750; and directors of accounting and auditing earned between $66,750 and $197,500 a year. The variation in salaries reflects differences in size of firm, location, level of education, and professional credentials.

Based on a survey by the Institute of Management Accountants, the average salary of IMA members was about $87,108 a year in 2003. IMA members who were certified public accountants averaged $95,031, while members who were certified management accountants averaged $89,200.

## Career Outlook

With the development of more sophisticated and flexible accounting systems, management accountants are taking on greater advisory roles and focusing more on analyzing operations rather than just providing financial data. Demand for internal auditors has increased in recent years due to the focus on risk management.

The outlook for the profession is good. Job openings arise as a result of growth and as accountants retire or transfer to other occupations.

According to the *Jobs Rated Almanac*, accountant ranked as the fifth best overall occupation among 250 occupations when judged on the criteria of work environment, job security, stress, income, career outlook, and physical demands. As for job outlook, accounting ranked thirty-third overall. This rating was negatively affected by the increased automation of the accounting function.

As the economy grows, firms and businesses will require more accountants to set up their books, prepare taxes, and offer management advice. Changes in legislation related to taxes, financial reporting standards, business investments, mergers, and other financial transactions also require businesses to engage the services of accountants.

In spite of these opportunities, competition for the most prestigious jobs is keen. Many accounting graduates are pursuing CMA and CIA certifica-

---

### HELP WANTED: SENIOR FINANCIAL ANALYST

Our radio station is seeking a detail-oriented professional to be responsible for weekly and monthly reporting requirements. This will include statements covering market share, weekly profit and loss, sports analysis, and accounts receivable. In addition, the professional will assist with tax packages, participate in the annual budget process, and complete other related duties as assigned. The qualified candidate will possess a B.A. in accounting and have at least three years of accounting experience, preferably in broadcasting or a related field. Applicant must demonstrate strong analytical skills and work well under deadlines. For immediate consideration, send résumé, salary history, and letter of interest.

tions rather than a CPA, so competition could be greater in management accounting than in public accounting. Also, due to the increasing popularity of tax preparation firms and software, accountants will shift away from tax preparation.

## Strategy for Finding the Jobs

The most common avenue for securing a position is still through college placement offices, so be sure to be knowledgeable about and take full advantage of what your college has to offer. Companies looking for accounting professionals often conduct campus interviews or prescreenings on campus.

Other avenues to pursue include Internet job banks that list industry and business accounting and auditing jobs. Want ads in papers and trade journals often list numerous openings. In addition, job seekers may also seek out firms that offer accounting and auditing services. If there are no openings immediately, perhaps they will keep your résumé on file in case an opening comes up.

Once in college, you should join several professional associations. As an association member, you will meet others who may help you find employment. Don't forget that networking is probably the most important route to landing a job. Tell everyone you come in contact with that you are (or will be) looking for a job. Perhaps others can put you in touch with a job possibility or with someone else who can give you the lead that will eventually materialize into a job.

## Management Accounting in Canada

In Canada, management accountants work in all types of organizations—finance, insurance, business services, retail and wholesale trade, and more. These professionals are knowledgeable in accounting and overall business practices.

The rigorous CMA accreditation, discussed earlier in this chapter, is sought by those management accountants who wish to improve their marketability and to enhance their skills in financial matters, leadership, decision making, and business expertise. Sample competencies required are in the areas of strategic planning, human resources management, risk management, and benchmarking. The certification process begins with completing a university degree that includes courses in management studies, general accounting studies, and related studies, such as economics and business law. Candidates must then pass an entrance exam followed by a two-year leadership program and work experience. CMAs work at all levels in varied organizations. In the last decade, CMAs have doubled in number, and that number continues to grow.

Management accountants may seek the CA designation, highlighted in Chapter 6. Optional specialization areas of interest to the management accountant include internal auditing and information systems auditing. CAs work in many management capacities, up to and including CEO positions.

The Department of Human Resources Development Canada reports that the average earnings for accountants are above the average for all jobs, and the rate of growth in earnings is nearly double that of the average. The unemployment rate is below the average of all job types. Although the growth in employment opportunities for accountants is expected to be below average, organizations' need for business and accounting systems analysts will increase the demand for management accountants.

Accountants typically use employment agencies to aid in the job search. Websites of professional associations are another source for job listings. Accountants with a lot of computer experience have an advantage in the hiring process. Also in demand are those with skills in taxation, cost accounting, and new business development. New college graduates should take advantage of job recruiters at their universities, who seek accountants for junior positions.

## Professional Associations

**CMA Canada**
Mississauga Executive Centre
One Robert Speck Pkwy., Suite 1400
Mississauga, ON L4Z 3M3
Canada
cma-canada.org

**Financial Accounting Foundation (FAF)**
401 Merritt 7
P.O. Box 5116
Norwalk, CT 06856-5116
fasb.org/faf

**Financial Executives International (FEI)**
200 Campus Dr.
P.O. Box 1938
Florham Park, NJ 07932
fei.org

**Institute of Internal Auditors (IIA)**
249 Maitland Ave.
Altamonte Springs, FL 32701
theiia.org

**Institute of Management Accountants (IMA)**
10 Paragon Dr.
Montvale, NJ 07645
imanet.org

**National Association of State Auditors, Comptrollers and Treasurers**
   **(NASACT)**
2401 Regency Rd., Suite 302
Lexington, KY 40503-2914
nasact.org

# Interviews with Professionals

Management accounting jobs cover a broad array of responsibilities and specializations. The four interviews that follow provide a glimpse into the variety of employment opportunities that exist for management accountants.

## Meet Topé Oluwolé

Topé Oluwolé earned an associate in science degree in business administration (management concentration) and then went on to study computer science at both the University of Massachusetts and Northeastern University in Boston. He now serves as Management Accountant II at State Street Bank and Trust Company in Quincy, Massachusetts. He previously worked in customer service for the accounts payable department at Bolt, Beranek, and Newman, Inc. (in Cambridge, Massachusetts) in a temporary capacity.

"My work at Bolt, Beranek, and Newman taught me how different business and accounting cycles worked," he says. "I also learned how to solve problems that arose in different business scenarios.

"I started my management accountant position in April of 1993. This was when I made the official change from temporary to permanent work. I came to work at State Street's international securities operations department as my fourth temporary position at the bank. I did computer work (Excel spreadsheets and Word projects) for the vice president of the department. Two major projects, the International Operating Model and Request for Proposal, introduced me to the concept of my future management accountant position.

"The International Operating Model explained the flow of international securities transactions as they related to State Street and their international counterparts (their subcustodians). The Request for Proposal explained to banks in the Americas, Europe, and Asia-Pacific region what qualities State Street was looking for in a subcustodian.

"At that time, I had just finished the computer science curriculums at the University of Massachusetts and Northeastern, respectively. However, I was faced with some serious cognitive dissonance. I wanted a career, but I also wanted a degree. So I faced the dilemma of full-time work versus full-time school.

"When I was offered a permanent position at the bank, I told the hiring manager it would have to be nights because I planned on going back to school full-time. She said that was fine.

"I loved the international aspect of the business. To me, my job felt like a James Bond movie. I was the hero with a problem to solve, such as 'Why is this account out of balance?' My problem usually involved contacting exotic countries like France, Sweden, Malaysia, or Singapore, if their bank was responsible. I had some cool weapons—a cash transaction system that international banks and I could browse simultaneously to reconcile cash discrepancies.

"The most hectic period was at the end of the month, because in essence I did a summary of the month's work in one day. My group had a mandatory overtime period of at least six hours in addition to our normal shift.

"My job involved booking daily transactions and reconciling balances of my subcustodian countries' accounts. Each accountant had a mixture of subcustodian countries based on their experience, the number of transactions the subcustodian had, and how hard it was to resolve cash discrepancies.

"Each subcustodian had a list of mutual funds it sold or bought into. Those funds had their securities. A subcustodian had anywhere from four to four hundred funds. I made sure the funds reported cleared and available cash balance (on the State Street international cash system) for any day was in line with what the subcustodian had on their books. If 94,000,000 Belgian francs on a cash statement showed up as 366,999 on the system, I had a lot of work to do.

"First I had to find out when the account went out of balance. Was it today? (Too easy, just look at today's transactions.) Was it last year? If so, I would have to backtrack to find the statement where the account was last in balance with the system. When I found the statement (not finding a discrepancy was never an option), I would proceed forward to pinpoint how the account went out of balance. Did the French subcustodian book a trade late? Did I forget to book interest? Did someone else who may have processed my subcustodian's statement book an amount incorrectly to the system? Did a broker dealing in Singapore dollars make a lot of bad trades? Was the mutual fund group at fault? Did the subcustodian make trades it did not send statements for? Every day was something different.

"I loved talking to my counterparts in Singapore and Japan. They were always so timely with the information I needed. It was funny explaining to a manager in France that my French wasn't that good, only to find out that the subcustodian had written in English, but with bad penmanship.

"I also loved experiencing culture and commerce in other parts of the world. Back then (before the World Wide Web boom), the average person didn't get that kind of global exposure in an eight-hour shift.

"To be successful, I've always believed you have to have a balance of real-world experience and conventional postsecondary education. If you're savvy enough to do them simultaneously as I did, then you will also be successful.

"Also, throw away the typical definition of *accountant*. Because of what I had been taught an accountant was, I swore I would never ever become one. I ended up in an accounting department by accident, but I wasn't the stereotypical bookkeeper. I was James Bond."

## Meet Betty Fisher

Betty Fisher earned her associate in science degree from Goldey Beacom College and a D.E. in accounting. She is now a consultant on staff at the company Accounting with Computers located in Pittsburgh, Pennsylvania.

"I took an accounting class in high school and it became like a game. I enjoyed it took another accounting class the following year, and discovered that I did very well. I then went on to college for accounting," she says.

"My present job was attractive to me because it combined my accounting background with my management information systems (MIS) background," she says. "I install, train, implement, and troubleshoot accounting software. My job is to assist clients with conversions and upgrades. I create custom reports, fix problems when they occur, and teach customers how to use the software. It's busy, but at least I don't have the stress of covering payrolls and payroll taxes. I no longer have to worry about handling someone else's funds as I did when I was employed as a controller. The company I work for is a nicely mixed group where we all fit together like a fine machine.

"I like the creativity that the job offers. No one's accounting system works like anyone else's, and it's my job to get them up and running smoothly. It really is quite rewarding to watch the light shine in someone's face when they finally understand how it all fits together. The only downside is that the pay is not quite what I made as a controller."

Betty's advice to others considering an accounting career is to be open and very flexible.

### Meet Kerry L. Bennett

Kerry L. Bennett earned a bachelor of science in business administration (emphasis in administrative management) in 1987. She also attended a number of training seminars. She is now on staff at Wausau Insurance Companies in Overland Park, Kansas, as a field auditor.

"My job is relatively busy. On a typical day, I start by leaving the house at 8:00 A.M. and going to a place of business to conduct an audit. I will typically schedule two audits a day, which will usually get me home at 3:30 P.M. or so. I will then work at home until approximately 4:30 P.M.," she says.

"I usually work forty hours a week. The work atmosphere depends on the location from which I am operating. It can be relaxed working at home or more rigid working at another place of business.

"The aspect I like most about my job is the ability to schedule my own work and the luxury of working at home (telecommuting). The aspect I like least is the feeling of not knowing many people I work with. Also, traveling can represent a substantial percentage of my job, so being away from home is definitely a downside. However, I enjoy working with numbers and people, and being able to control my own schedule."

When considering a field in accounting, you must recognize that some jobs can require a lot of travel and working independent of others in your firm, either in your home or in clients' offices. Be sure you are honest with yourself about whether or not you would find these working conditions desirable.

### Meet Kelly Holmes

Kelly Holmes earned a bachelor of arts degree in accounting from the University of Missouri–Columbia in 1989. She is a CPA and senior accounting manager at Coca-Cola Bottling Company of Mid-America in Leraxa, Kansas (a division of Coca-Cola Enterprises in Atlanta, Georgia). Previously, she spent three and a half years in public accounting at the offices of Ernst & Young.

"I am in middle management and spend a lot of time delegating projects and reviewing," she says. "My job requires a lot of operational knowledge of how the business works. I oversee general ledger cost accounting, inventory, fixed assets, capital, expenditures, and payroll.

"Of all aspects of the job, I most enjoy working with all levels of employees and the many departments who oversee other applications. My least favorite aspect is the lack of time to properly train sales employees about financial knowledge.

"I feel that understanding financial impact is a challenge. I'd advise all those interested in this career to educate themselves in the areas of public speaking (presentations), computer software, and financial analysis."

# 8

# Path 3: Government Accounting

*"The legitimate object of government is to do for a community of people, whatever they need to have done, but cannot do at all, or cannot so well do for themselves, in their separate and individual capacities."*
—ABRAHAM LINCOLN

Government accounting attracts those graduates and experienced accountants who want to use their management accounting skills in a different setting. Though government agencies tend to pay less than private industry, government positions offer distinct advantages, including job security, excellent benefits, and some unique opportunities. The goal of the accounting department of a typical government agency is to function within the budgetary constraints mandated by legislative action.

## Definition of the Career Path

Many accountants, both CPAs and non-CPAs, are employed by a number of governmental agencies at federal, state, and local levels. Similar to public accounting and management accounting, these positions involve general accounting skills and specialization in more narrowly defined areas.

Government accountants and auditors perform a variety of duties, maintaining and examining the records of government agencies and auditing private businesses and individuals whose activities are subject to government regulations or taxation. This involves preparing the nation's budget, auditing public utilities, studying the background of bankruptcy, examining the books of stock exchange firms, and reviewing amounts spent by various governmental agencies.

They complete reports of examinations and, if appropriate, make arrangements to collect taxes due; ensure that the proper forms are filed by the individuals or businesses; assess any penalties for nonconformance to government regulations; and advise when prosecution should be considered. Government accountants also examine the financial records of banking institutions and securities exchanges and brokers. Accountants who work for the government—federal, state, or local—guarantee that revenues are received and expenditures are made in accordance with laws and regulations.

In a government department or agency, major concerns are budgets and grants. Since funds come from an appropriating source, requests must be detailed and precise. Accountants may be responsible for showing where matching funds will come from, exactly how a community stands to benefit, and statistics on the people it involves.

The accountant's prior work experience plays a large role in determining the types of job assignments. Training is provided for those lacking prior governmental accounting experience.

Advancement in the federal government is commonly based on a system of occupational levels, or grades, which have designated codes, such as GS-9 or GS-12. Workers enter the federal civil service at the starting grade for an occupation and, assuming their job performance is acceptable, are promoted until they reach the highest grade for their occupation. In this system, there are a limited number of noncompetitive promotions. Once nonsupervisory personnel reach the full-performance level of their career track, they usually receive periodic step increases within their grade, again assuming job performance is satisfactory. Beyond that, workers must compete for subsequent promotion, and advancement becomes more difficult.

## Opportunities at the Federal Level

Following are a few of the numerous accounting-related job possibilities in the federal government.

**Revenue Officer.** Revenue officers collect delinquent taxes, investigate business situations, negotiate agreements in order to satisfy tax obligations, and perform other tasks to safeguard the government's interests. Revenue officers who enter government employment with a bachelor's degree start at the GS-5 or GS-7 level.

**Budget Analyst.** The budget analyst determines how to allocate funds to various agencies. Job responsibilities involve studying previous budgets, reviewing department requests, and ascertaining the level of resources needed to perform various functions.

**Internal Revenue Service Agent.** The Internal Revenue Service is one of the largest employers of accountants in the United States. IRS agents examine and audit the accounting books and records of individuals, businesses, and corporations to determine their correct federal tax liabilities. Additionally, the agents conduct compliance examinations regarding technical requirements of the Internal Revenue Code. Candidates must have a CPA certificate, or they must have a four-year college degree in accounting, or an equivalent combination of at least thirty semester hours of accounting education and work experience. Entry-level positions will be at the GS-5, GS-7, or GS-9 level, depending on the education level attained and previous experience.

Working as an IRS agent requires strong accounting abilities, good planning and organizational skills, and competence in oral and written communications.

**Chief Bank Examiner.** A chief bank examiner investigates financial institutions to enforce laws and regulations governing the institutions. The examiner schedules audits, evaluates examination reports, and confers with the institutions' officials, with financial advisors, and with regulatory officials.

## Opportunities at the State Level
States also have a need for qualified financial advisors. CPAs in state government have the opportunity to evaluate the efficiency of government departments and agencies. At the state level, a CPA may be a member of a team assessing the adequacy of the investment portfolio of the treasurer's office. Also at this level, government accountants may work for the Department of Audit and Control or the Department of Taxation and Finance as accountants, auditors, or tax examiners, from entry-level to senior positions.

## Opportunities at the Local Level
At the city and local government level, individuals may be employed as accountants, staff accountants, or accountant administrators.

## Possible Job Titles

Accountant
Accounting supervisor
Agency fiscal officer
Assistant accountant
Assistant auditor
Assistant controller
Audit manager
Auditor

## SAMPLE FEDERAL GOVERNMENT JOB POSTING

Vacancy Announcement: Department of Justice—Bureau of Prisons/Federal
Prison System

Vacancy Announcement Number: 04-GIL-DEU-016

Position: Accountant GS-0510-05/07/09

Salary: $32,933.00 to $53,940.00 PA (Includes law enforcement and locality)

Promotion Potential: GS-09

Duty Location: 1 vacancy at FCI Gilmer (UNICOR), Glenville, West Virginia

Applications will be accepted from: Open to all qualified persons

Selection will be made without discrimination for any nonmerit reason such as
race, color, religion, sex, sexual orientation, national origin, age, physical
disability, marital status, parental status, or membership in an employee
organization.

### Major Duties

Supervises and directs the maintenance of all corporation type accounting
records for the UNICOR Factory and assists the Business Manager in
maintaining records. The records include a complete set of accounts consisting
of real accounts, nominal accounts, statistical accounts, and various construction
and vocational accounts that are subject to budgetary limitations.

Responsible for the maintenance of the double-entry accounting cycle, which
consists of the following essential operations: posting, journalizing, taking trial
balances, determining necessary end-of-period adjustments, making
reconciliations, preparing worksheets, adjusting and closing the books, taking
pre- and postclosing trial balances, and preparing the accounting statements and
statement analysis.

Incumbent participates in the management of the operating program by
supplying accounting and financial statements, reports, and other information of
a factual nature, including other standard types of statements and reports,
including such data as job analysis of manufacturing statements, summary
analysis of the Washington control accounting transactions, etc. Provides
interpretations of accounting reports, statements, and data that point out
trends or liaisons with operating and management officials at all levels to
ascertain their needs for accounting data to ensure that those needs are being
met.

**Qualifications Required**

Per Office of Personnel Management (OPM) Qualification Standards for General Schedule Positions Operating Manual: Accounting, GS-0510 series; and the Group Coverage Qualification Standard for Professional and Scientific Positions.

**Basic Requirements**

Accounting degree; a four-year course of study leading to a bachelor's degree in accounting; or a degree in a related field such as business administration, finance, or public administration that included or was supplemented by 24 semester hours in accounting. The 24 hours may include up to 6 hours of credit in business law. Applicants who meet the criteria for Superior Academic Achievement qualify for positions at the GS-07 level.

Or, a combination of education and experience—at least four years of experience in accounting, or an equivalent combination of accounting experience, college-level education, and training that provided professional accounting knowledge. The applicant's background must include one of the following:

1. Twenty-four semester hours in accounting or auditing courses of appropriate type and quality. This can include up to six hours of business law;
2. A certificate as a Certified Public Accountant or a Certificate Internal Auditor, obtained through written examination; or
3. Completion of the requirements for a degree that included substantial course work in accounting or auditing, e.g., 15 semester hours, but that does not fully satisfy the 24-semester-hours requirement, provided that (a) the applicant successfully worked in the full performance level of accounting, auditing, or a related field; (b) a panel of two professional accountants or auditors has determined that the applicant has demonstrated a good knowledge of accounting and related fields that equals the successful completion of the four-year course of study in accounting.

In addition to meeting the basic requirements, applicants must meet the following:

General Experience: None

Specialized Experience: GS-07: One full academic year of graduate education or law school or superior academic achievement OR one year of specialized experience equivalent to at least the GS-05 level. GS-09: two full academic

*continued*

years of progressively higher level graduate education or master's or equivalent graduate degree or L.L.B. or J.D. OR one year of specialized experience equivalent to at least the GS-07 level.

Equivalent combinations of education and experience are qualifying for all grade levels for which both education and experience are acceptable.

Note: Basic qualifications are determined solely from information submitted on application and/or résumé. Do not generalize experience on your résumé, or OF-612.

Applicants meeting basic eligibility requirements will be rated and ranked on responses to the KSAs (Knowledge, Skills, and Abilities) required to perform the duties of the position. KSA responses should include applicable experience, objectives of work, and evidence of success. Credit will be given for unpaid experience or volunteer work, such as community, cultural, social service, and professional association activities on the same basis as for paid work experience. To receive proper credit you must show the actual time, such as number of hours per week spent in the activities.

**Basis of Rating**

For CTAP and ICTAP, *well-qualified* means that the applicant meets the qualification standard and eligibility requirements for the position, meets minimum educational and experience requirements, meets all selective factors where applicable, and is able to satisfactorily perform the duties of the position upon entry.

**How to Apply**

Applicants within the Federal Bureau of Prisons must submit:

1. Position Application Form (BP-153-23)
2. A copy of your most recent performance evaluation (not more than 13 months old)
3. An Optional Application for Federal Employment (OF-612), or Application for Federal Employment (SF-171/172), or a résumé that follows the instructions of the OPM Flyer "Applying for a Federal Job" (OF-510)
4. Responses for the identified knowledge, skills, and abilities (KSAs)
5. A qualification inquiry form regarding convictions of misdemeanor crimes of domestic violence (if not currently in a primary law enforcement position)
6. A copy of your most recent Notification of Personnel Action (SF-50B)
7. A Qualification Rating Form (BP-508)
8. A copy of College Transcript

Applicants outside the Federal Bureau of Prisons (i.e., CTAP eligibles) must submit:

1. An Optional Application for Federal Employment (OF-612), or Application for Federal Employment (SF-171/172), or a résumé that follows the instructions of the OPM Flyer "Applying for a Federal Job" (OF-510)
2. A copy of your most recent performance evaluation (not more than 13 months old)
3. Responses for the identified knowledge, skills, and abilities (KSAs)
4. A copy of your most recent Notification of Personnel Action (SF-50B)
5. A copy of College Transcript

Budget analyst
Budget director
City finance manager
Controller
County treasurer
Credit union examiner
Director, accounting services
Finance systems analyst
Financial officer
General Accounting Office accountant
Internal Revenue Service agent
Internal Revenue Service tax specialist
Junior accountant
Junior auditor
Operating accountant
Revenue officer
Securities and Exchange Commission
    accountant
Securities investigator
Senior accountant
Senior commodities tax examiner
Staff accountant
State treasurer
Supervisory staff accountant
Systems accountant
Tax examiner
Tax technician

## Possible Employers

The federal government system consists of fifteen cabinet departments and more than ninety independent agencies. These departments and agencies, which vary in size, have offices all over the world. The larger the agency, the more diverse are the possibilities for accountants. However, many smaller agencies and departments also employ government accountants. In the federal government, the Treasury Department, which includes the IRS, employs large numbers of accounting professionals.

For those who like to travel, government jobs offer abundant opportunities to relocate within the fifty states and throughout the world. Employment positions exist abroad for more than 50,000 U.S. citizens.

Opportunities at state and local levels vary, but the greatest need for accountants is normally found in the larger departments and agencies, such as those handling transportation and road maintenance, law enforcement, and tax collection.

## Related Occupations

Related careers include commodity analyst, estate planner, fiscal analyst, investment analyst, financial officer, bond analyst, securities analyst, loan officer, and tax consultant.

## Working Conditions

Accountants who work for government agencies generally work in comfortable office environments. They may have private offices or work in large office areas. Those working in government agencies usually work between thirty-five and forty hours per week. Working for certain government agencies might require extensive national and international travel to audit government facilities.

## Training and Qualifications

During high school, you should complete a college preparatory academic program, including courses in English, mathematics, social studies, and the biological and physical sciences. Electives in business practices, accounting, economics, and data processing also should be included. Concentrate on building strengths in oral and written communications and in mathematics. If you take introductory accounting, you should understand that initially you will concentrate on fundamentals, not broad concepts.

A bachelor's degree in accounting or a related field is the recommended undergraduate program for persons planning on entering this profession. The federal government requires four years of college (including twenty-four semester hours in accounting or auditing) or an equivalent combination of education and experience for its beginning accounting and auditing positions. In addition to taking liberal arts courses in English, government, mathematics, biological and physical sciences, social sciences, and humanities, students majoring in accounting normally complete courses in computer applications, finance, economics, and business law. Professional courses in your program should cover such areas as the organization of the profession; ethics and professional responsibilities; financial, managerial, and governmental accounting; auditing; and taxation.

Many colleges and universities offer master's degree programs in accounting. Some universities have a professional school or program of accounting that sets forth at least two years of preprofessional preparation and three years of progressively more advanced professional-level studies. While a few states permit candidates to sit for the CPA examination upon earning a baccalaureate degree, most require college work beyond the bachelor's degree.

Success as a government accountant requires above-average intelligence, high mathematical aptitude, a liking for detailed work, and strong communication skills. You should have a logical, analytical approach to solving problems and be able to work without direct supervision. Accuracy in work habits, integrity, and ambition are important qualifications. You also should be able to make decisions and concentrate on a problem for long periods of time.

The Association of Government Accountants grants the Certified Government Financial Manager (CGFM) designation for accountants, auditors, and other government financial personnel at the federal, state, and local levels. Candidates must have a minimum of a bachelor's degree, twenty-four hours of study in financial management, and two years' experience in government. Candidates must also pass a series of three exams. The exams cover topics in governmental environment; governmental accounting, financial reporting, and budgeting; and financial management and control.

Many government jobs require extensive entry-level training. For example, if you are employed as an IRS agent, you begin with classroom training that covers tax law, fraud examination, and research techniques. Then, under the guidance of professionals, you continue your training on the job. Next comes classroom and computer-based training on more complex areas of business and individual tax returns. Continuing education opportunities are provided throughout your career as a revenue agent. As you progress, you might remain a tax generalist, specialize in the returns of a particular industry, or be called upon to instruct new trainees. Investigations or special projects might also require your participation.

## Earnings

Earnings of government workers at the federal level are somewhat lower than for accountants in other areas. In 2004, the starting annual salary for junior accountants and auditors was $24,075, the GS-5 rate. New hires with a GS-7 rating start at $29,821. Those with a master's degree or two years of experience start at a GS-9 level, which pays $36,478 per year. Top earnings for a GS-9 accountant are $47,422 per year. Employees with a GS-11 ranking start at $44,136. Salaries were up to 21 percent higher in selected areas where the prevailing local pay level was higher. You should also note that GS pay is adjusted geographically, and the majority of jobs pay a higher salary than those listed. Exact pay information can be found on position vacancy announcements.

Accountants employed by the federal government in nonsupervisory, supervisory, and managerial positions averaged $69,370 a year in 2003; auditors averaged $73,247.

In addition to base pay and bonuses, federal employees may receive incentive awards. These one-time awards, ranging from $25 to $10,000, are bestowed for a significant suggestion, a special act or service, or sustained high job performance. Some workers also may receive premium pay, which is granted when the employee must work overtime, on holidays, on weekends, at night, or under hazardous conditions.

All employees receive ten paid holidays. Vacation time is paid at a rate of thirteen days per year for the first three years, twenty days per year with three to fifteen years' service, and twenty-six days per year after fifteen years. Additionally, thirteen sick days are accrued each year regardless of length of service. Military time counts toward benefits. If you have three years of military service, for example, you begin with four weeks of paid vacation and have accrued three years toward retirement.

In 2002, median annual earnings for accountants and auditors in state government were $42,680. In local government, the median earnings were $44,690.

## Career Outlook

Through the year 2012, employment of accountants and auditors is expected to grow about as fast as the average for all occupations, which is 10 to 20 percent. In an effort to make government agencies more efficient and accountable, demand for government accountants should increase. Uncle Sam employs more than 1,900,000 civilian workers. The U.S. government is the largest employer in the United States, hiring 1.3 percent of the nation's civilian workforce.

## Strategy for Finding the Jobs

Similar to private industry, many federal agencies fill their jobs by allowing applicants to contact the agency directly for job information and application processing. Résumés are preferred when applying; however, the Optional Application for Federal Employment, OF 612, is also accepted. Most positions do not require a written test. While the process is similar to that in private industry, there are differences due to the laws, executive orders, and regulations that govern federal employment.

USAJOBS is the federal government's official Employment Information System. It is operated by the U.S. Office of Personnel Management (OPM). On USAJOBS online (usajobs.opm.gov), you can explore more than fifteen thousand jobs on any given day; build and store up to five résumés for applying to federal jobs; and access a wide range of information about federal agencies and federal employment issues. USAJOBS is also accessible by telephone (703-724-1850 or TDD 978-461-8404).

An agency is required to post its competitive service positions on OPM's USAJOBS system whenever the agency is seeking applicants from the general public and outside of the agency. Competitive service jobs are those that are subject to the civil service laws passed by Congress to ensure that applicants and employees receive fair and equal treatment in the hiring process. Many agencies also post their excepted service positions on USAJOBS. Excepted service positions are within agencies that set their own qualification requirements and are not subject to the civil service laws.

Agencies' job postings on USAJOBS include all of the instructions and procedures for applying to that particular position. Follow the instructions very carefully. Omitted information can result in your application not being evaluated. Many announcements allow applicants to apply online directly to the agencies. In the future, you will be able to track your application status for each of your applications.

After your application is received, your qualifications and test results (if required) are evaluated and you are given a numerical rating. The higher your rating, the more likely you'll be contacted for further information or an interview. Applicants who do not meet the minimum qualifications will not be considered.

For further assistance in your job search with the federal government and to learn more about the various agencies, review the following publications at your local library:

- *The United States Government Manual*—This book provides agency descriptions, addresses, contacts, and basic employment information.
- *Guide to America's Federal Jobs*—This guide shows you how to find and apply for federal jobs.

Application requirements with smaller government bodies vary. Contact state or local government personnel agencies to discover their needs for applicants.

## Government Accounting in Canada

One in ten financial auditors and accountants in Canada works in public administration, according to the Department of Human Resources Development Canada. Some of these professionals have CA certification. CAs work in jobs in all levels of the government, including tax auditors, financial analysts, and the influential positions of auditors general and deputy ministers. As in private industry, CAs in the government are recognized for their leadership and management abilities.

Job openings and application procedures for federal government employment are available online. Via the Government of Canada website (canada .gc.ca), applicants can access job openings of the various agencies and departments of the federal government. The job postings give specific details on candidates' required qualifications and the application procedures. The site of the Public Service Commission of Canada (accessible on the government website or at http://jobs.gc.ca) has information on jobs open to the public and jobs for new university graduates. These job postings provide job descriptions; education, work experience, and other requirements; work environment; and job challenges.

# Professional Associations

**Association of Government Accountants (AGA)**
2208 Mount Vernon Ave.
Alexandria, VA 22301
agacgfm.org

**Government Finance Officers Association (GFOA)**
203 N. LaSalle St., Suite 2700
Chicago, IL 60601-1210
gfoa.org

# Interview with a Professional

The government accountant introduced here was fortunate to be in the right place at the right time. His work history illustrates one way it is possible for the professional accountant to advance from entry-level to high-level government accounting work.

### Meet Barry Faison

Barry Faison earned his B.S. in accounting from Virginia Commonwealth University in Richmond, Virginia, in 1975 and earned his M.S., also from Virginia Commonwealth, in business accounting in 1976. He also holds CPA and certified government financial manager (CGFM) credentials and currently serves as a controller for the Virginia Retirement System in Richmond, Virginia.

"I began my career working for the Commonwealth of Virginia's Auditor of Public Accounts during my last semester at VCU," he says. "At the time, certification as a CPA in Virginia involved passing the exam and having two years of auditing experience with a CPA firm or four years with a governmental auditing agency.

"My interest in accounting began as an interest in math," he says. "During my first year and a half at VCU, my major was math education (I had hoped to teach math). I left VCU to go into the army, and spent the next three and a half years in the service. I returned to VCU and changed my major to math (I had decided that I really didn't want to teach by that time).

"I decided that I needed to have a more practical application for my interest in numbers and enrolled in an introductory accounting class. The class material and the instructor provided me the direction I needed to focus my interest.

"My father worked at a bank in Richmond for most of his career. My great-uncle spent his career as a bookkeeper for a Richmond leather company. I think that these people influenced my initial interest in numbers and its related fields. However, it was my instructors at VCU who helped me finally decide on accounting as a career.

"I did not have any other related work experience before graduating from college. My first employment after college was with the Commonwealth of Virginia's Auditor of Public Accounts. This job gave me a variety of auditing experiences, including serving with a number of different agencies of the commonwealth and several other local governments.

"My last auditing assignment there led to landing my current position. During my previous assignment as one of the auditors on the audit of the Virginia Retirement System, a number of weaknesses and problems were noted. Because of the condition of the records, a 'balance sheet' audit was done and the report was issued with the audited balance sheet and a number of 'management points.' The Joint Legislative Audit and Review Commission (JLARC), an agency of the legislature, reviewed the agency operations and concluded that the agency should have additional 'professional' accounting staff and an internal audit department. I applied for and was hired to fill one of those positions.

"During approximately twenty years with the Virginia Retirement System, I have served as accounting supervisor, accounting manager, and the agency controller. In the span of that time, I have become accustomed to how most of the finance department works.

"My current position makes me responsible for three major departments within the System (member records, general ledger and financial reporting, and control). I spend most of my day either in meetings or working on a computer. Work in meetings involves problem resolution or planning. The computer work involves word processing—writing procedures and policies and general correspondence with participating employers and spreadsheets—designing forms, analyzing accounts, and preparing financial statements.

"The job involves having a number of different projects going on simultaneously. This means that tasks have to be evaluated and prioritized, and that sometimes there are more tasks than time. In a typical day, I spend a lot of my time dealing with exceptions. Unless I am involved in the installation of a new system or a special project, I do not usually work on the same thing two days in a row. The bulk of the recordkeeping and reporting are delegated to staff who have responsibility for specific tasks.

"Routinely, I meet with the finance department managers and other department managers to coordinate current work and plan for process changes. I prepare spreadsheets analyzing the financial statement information and quarterly reports that include financial information from the general ledger, statistical information from the employer reporting and member records systems, and compliance information concerning the timeliness of reconciliations, employer reporting, and contributions payments. I represent the System in meetings with other agencies of the Commonwealth on issues that relate to the interfaces with the System and/or new or revised requirements being proposed for the System. I am also responsible for working with the external auditors during their annual audit of the System. During the month of August, I am involved with the preparation of the financial section of the System's annual report and may work fifty to sixty hours each week, some of which is at home.

"The aspects of my work that I like most are the variety and flexibility. Because of my position, I am involved in all areas of the finance department and play a role in coordinating work with other departments. This allows me to do a number of different types of work each day. I like having the opportunity to be creative in developing solutions to financial recordkeeping and reporting problems. On the downside, routine administrative tasks are what I like least about my work."

How can accountants find the success Barry has? (1) Learn areas besides accounting and business, such as technology. Perhaps even learn a programming language. The logic involved helps in overall organization, and the knowledge helps in working with information systems staff. (2) Throughout your career, pursue opportunities for additional education and professional certification. Continuing education keeps you abreast of the latest in the accounting field and keeps you prepared for a job change, should one be desired or necessary.

# 9

# Path 4:
# Accounting Education

*"A teacher affects eternity; he can never tell where his influence stops."*
—HENRY ADAMS

Many first or second graders confess that they want to be teachers when they grow up. Some people arrive at this career decision a bit later in life. In some cases, it is the rewarding nature of the profession that is the attraction; for others it is the atmosphere, which is both stimulating and challenging. Still others enjoy the intellectual pursuits and professional stature afforded teachers. Many individuals feel they are making a contribution not only to the individuals they work with directly but to society as a whole.

Certainly teaching has many rewards. But it can also be difficult, demanding work. And as a rule, most teachers will tell you that it wasn't monetary remuneration that prompted them to choose this career. Is teaching for you?

Ask yourself the following questions:

1. Is patience one of my virtues?
2. Do I enjoy working with people?
3. Am I confident about all the subject areas in my field?
4. Am I willing and able to put in the necessary hours? (Many hours are required for planning, grading papers, attending meetings, and remaining current in the field.)
5. Do I have the skills required to perform ably in front of a group?
6. Am I capable of maintaining discipline?
7. Do I have sufficient enthusiasm for teaching?
8. Am I creative enough to develop new approaches for students who learn in different ways?
9. Is an educational setting attractive to me?

**HELP WANTED: EDUCATOR**

The Department of Accounting and Finance at a state university is seeking candidates for a tenure-track position for next fall. Doctorate in accounting/A.B.D. (all but dissertation) candidates nearing completion may also be considered. Applicants will be judged on their potential for excellence in research and teaching, although preference will be given to applicants who can submit completed research. The college offers undergraduate and M.B.A. programs. Application review will begin immediately and continue until the position is filled. Please send your cover letter, résumé, and names and addresses of three references to the Chairman of the Department of Accounting and Finance.

Individuals who have been working in the accounting field are often drawn to this career because they want to use their knowledge and accounting experience to educate others. As long as accounting and financial management practices continue to become more and more complicated, accounting students will require a stronger education to prepare for their careers.

# Definition of the Career Path

Accounting teachers have opportunities at both the secondary and the postsecondary levels. Not only do the students vary between the two alternatives, but the work expectations differ as well.

## High School Teaching

Secondary school teachers work with a diverse group of students and must prepare lessons that meet the needs of this varied population. Teachers incorporate various instructional tools and methods in the classroom. One classroom aid is the computer—helping the students with learning and helping the teacher with instructional and administrative duties.

Outside of the classroom, teachers perform planning, evaluating, and administrative duties. Teachers may oversee study halls and supervise extracurricular activities.

There are many opportunities for professional development for teachers to learn new skills and enhance existing skills. In many schools, teachers are increasingly involved in site-based management, which involves them in decision making. After work experience as a classroom instructor and with additional preparation, teachers may move into positions as school librarians, administrators, supervisors, or mentor teachers. Competition is stiff for these advanced positions, which are usually few in number.

### College Teaching

Accounting educators are on the faculty of community and junior colleges, colleges of business administration, graduate schools of business, and schools of professional accountancy.

Business and community colleges offer a two-year degree that usually includes introductory courses in accounting principles, financial accounting, cost accounting, accounting for individual income taxes, and accounting systems. Teachers conduct several classes per day or per week, give and grade tests, and counsel students.

Community colleges may be part of a university system. Teachers employed in a university system will find situations similar to those at a university, and their responsibilities may well include research and publishing.

All staff members are expected to excel in teaching, to work with students in both general and specialized accounting courses, to contribute to the profession through serving on educational and professional committees, and to conduct research and prepare materials based upon their research. Other responsibilities include planning and assessing course objectives and curriculums, preparing lesson materials, presenting classroom lectures, assigning and supervising student course work and research projects, and evaluating student progress. Most faculty use computer technology extensively in all areas of their work.

At colleges and universities, educators often begin their careers as instructors. After obtaining advanced education and/or experience, instructors may advance to assistant professors, then associate professors, and eventually professors. For example, at four-year universities, it is preferred that associate professors have university-level teaching experience along with a doctorate degree.

An average teaching load is twelve to sixteen hours per week, not counting preparation time, staff conferences, and meetings. Classes may consist of anything from large numbers of students in lecture halls to much smaller groups (especially at the graduate level) where more individual attention may be provided. Professors often have teaching assistants (usually Ph.D. candidates) whom they must observe, evaluate, and supervise. Students are usually required to turn in essays, term papers, and other written work, which

## HELP WANTED: EDUCATOR

Our state university invites applications for one permanent, full-time (nine-month), tenure-track assistant professor of accounting position, which is anticipated to become available next year. Primary teaching interest should be financial accounting. The position requires a doctorate in accounting or A.B.D., an interest in and the ability to conduct research leading to publication, and the potential for successful teaching at both the undergraduate and graduate level. Six-hour teaching load, summer research support, competitive salary, and excellent fringe benefits are included. Send letter of application, résumé, dissertation proposal or a research paper, and three letters of recommendation.

educators must evaluate, grade, and return to students. In addition, teachers are expected to be available to advise students about career choices, courses, or other matters. This can translate into an additional three to six hours per week (usually slotted as office hours, during which teachers make themselves available to students on a regular basis). Staff members may also be called on to aid in special projects, internships, graduate theses, and registration; serve on department and university committees; and develop proposals for research grants. Those who become department heads have additional responsibilities. In addition to teaching, educators are usually expected to publish written work. Those who are employed at four-year institutions are expected to produce more than those who are on staff at community colleges. Teachers at community colleges are usually assigned a larger number of classes.

Accounting faculty are at the same time members of two professions—accounting and education. They bear the responsibilities and gain the rewards of both careers.

## Possible Job Titles

Adjunct staff member
Assistant professor
Associate professor
Department chair
Department head
Instructor
Lecturer

Professor
Program chair
Teacher
University educator

## Possible Employers

Teachers of accounting may find employment in public or private high schools, community or junior colleges, and public or private colleges and universities.

## Related Occupations

Occupations related to secondary school teachers are librarians, counselors, social workers, education administrators, and public relations specialists. These fields require attributes similar to those that make one a good teacher, for example, good communication skills, motivational skills, patience, creativity, and the ability and desire to work with youth.

### HELP WANTED: EDUCATOR

Our university is an independent accredited institution. We serve about five thousand students each year in undergraduate programs as well as maintain an evening M.B.A. program. The accounting program has approximately five hundred students and serves additional students who are enrolled in other majors. Responsibilities include teaching, professional development, university service, and providing leadership to full-time and adjunct faculty in the area of accounting. Teaching assignments will include undergraduate and pre-M.B.A. courses in accounting and finance. Contract faculty teach three trimesters from September through early August annually. Both excellence in teaching and university service and leadership are stressed. A master's degree in business administration or accounting, one or more relevant professional certifications (for example, CPA or CMA), recent relevant business experience as a CFO or equivalent, and teaching experience at the undergraduate level are required. Ph.D. in accounting preferred. Applications will be reviewed upon receipt. Interested individuals should submit a letter of application, résumé, and names of three references.

### HELP WANTED: EDUCATOR

Our small liberal arts international educational institution is in need of an additional accounting faculty member for next fall. Minimum requirement is an M.B.A. with a CPA. Terminal degree in business or related field is preferred. The candidate must have a commitment to teaching, interest in research, and an international education. Faculty members are appointed for multiyear contract terms. Curriculum vitae with cover letter and copy of transcripts may be sent to the director of personnel. Applications will be taken until the position is filled.

College and university faculty function both as teachers and researchers who communicate information and ideas.

## Working Conditions

Although some generalizations can be made about most teachers' working conditions, be aware that situations can differ significantly from one institution to another.

### High School Teaching

Although teaching can be very rewarding, dedicated secondary school teachers have a lot of stress—from heavy workloads, disruptive and unmotivated students, large class size, and lack of appropriate resources. The trend is for teachers to work more in teams than alone to help alleviate isolation and to increase professional development. One plus of being a teacher is the two-month break in the summer for most districts, although it may include the fulfillment of course work and other continuing education requirements. Staff of year-round schools get more but shorter breaks from instruction.

### College Teaching

Accountants teaching in colleges and universities have working conditions similar to other faculty members. They usually have offices in which they prepare teaching materials, study and write reports, do research, grade papers, write articles for publication, counsel students, and perform administrative duties. Other than being present for classes and regular office hours, college teachers have the choice of when, where, and how long to work.

Some postsecondary faculty teach night and weekend classes, especially teachers at two-year colleges or institutions with large enrollments of older students who have full-time jobs or family responsibilities. Most postsecondary teachers work nine months of the year. A growing number of college and university faculty work part-time. Some part-timers, or adjunct faculty, have primary jobs in other areas of accounting.

University faculty may find it hard to balance the responsibilities of teaching students with the pressure to conduct research and publish findings. Recent cutbacks and the hiring of more part-time faculty have put a greater administrative burden on full-time faculty. Requirements to teach online classes also have added greatly to the workloads of postsecondary teachers. Many find it very time-consuming to develop the courses, learn how to operate the technology, and answer large quantities of e-mail.

## Training and Qualifications

To obtain a good basis for future study, while in high school, follow college preparatory programs that contain as many courses in relevant business, accounting, and mathematics as possible.

### High School Teaching

Postsecondary education requirements for public high school teachers vary from state to state, but everyone must (1) earn a bachelor's degree from a college or university that has a state-approved curriculum and (2) be licensed. A significant number of Internet job postings for accounting teachers indicate that they must also teach other business courses and computer technology.

### HELP WANTED: EDUCATOR

Our Midwestern university is seeking to fill two positions in accounting. Rank is at either the assistant or the associate professor level. Appointment begins next fall. A Ph.D. or D.B.A. is required. Candidates for assistant professor must exhibit capacity for quality research and teaching. Candidates for associate professor must have an established record of excellence in research, teaching, and service on doctoral dissertation committees. Applications will be reviewed as they come in.

Some states require a minimum grade point average and training in technology. In some states, a master's degree is mandatory within a specified time period of beginning teaching. Once you have completed your studies, most states require that applicants for a teacher's license successfully pass a certification competency examination. These tests are designed to measure subject matter mastery, basic skills, and teaching capabilities. Nowadays, school systems are moving toward implementing performance-based systems for licensure, which usually require the teacher to demonstrate satisfactory teaching performance over an extended period in order to obtain a provisional license, in addition to passing an examination in one's subject. When certificates come up for renewal, additional course work may be required.

Many states allow you to teach at the high school level with a provisional certification immediately upon obtaining your accounting degree. Regular certification is attained by working with an experienced educator for one or two years while completing the necessary education courses.

As a teacher at the high school level, you may be employed by a private rather than public institution. Private schools are usually less stringent and often don't make state certification a requirement.

There are optional certifications available to teachers who wish to show advanced levels of competency. One such certification is available through the National Board for Professional Teaching Standards, which requires preparing a work portfolio and passing a written assessment.

Professional development schools, which partner with universities and secondary schools, are available in many states. Students enter these one-year programs after finishing their bachelor's degrees. In these schools, students teach for a year under professional guidance, putting their book knowledge into practice.

## College Teaching

Teaching at the college level usually requires a minimum of a master's degree. During graduate school, students generally specialize in a particular area of accounting. If you plan on completing a master's or doctorate degree program, contact the graduate schools you are interested in to obtain information on admission requirements so that you may plan your undergraduate program accordingly. Large numbers of doctorate-level educators will be found at four-year institutions.

A good way to gain college teaching experience is to become a graduate teaching assistant (TA). To qualify, you must be enrolled in a graduate school program. TAs usually work at the institutions and in the departments where they are earning their degrees, but teaching or internship positions for graduate students at institutions that do not grant graduate degrees have become more common recently.

A major step in the traditional academic career is the attainment of tenure. Newly hired faculty serve for a specific period (usually seven years) under term contracts. Their record of teaching, research, and overall contributions to the institution is then reviewed, and tenure is granted if the review is favorable and positions are available. Once an educator receives tenure, he or she is guaranteed a position on the faculty for life, unless there is a serious breach on his or her part.

Advancement for postsecondary teachers often involves a move into administrative and managerial positions, such as departmental chairperson, dean, and president. At four-year institutions, such advancement requires a doctoral degree. At two-year colleges, a doctorate is helpful but not usually required, except for advancement to some top administrative positions.

# Earnings

As is true with other accounting jobs, the accounting teachers' salary is determined by factors that include the job description, the individual's education and years of service, and the geographic region of employment.

### High School Teaching

In 2002, median annual earnings for secondary school teachers ranged from $39,810 to $44,340. According to the American Federation of Teachers, beginning teachers with a bachelor's degree earned an average of $30,719 in the 2001–2002 school year. Private school teachers generally earn less than public school teachers. Teachers can boost their salaries by coaching sports, working with students in extracurricular activities, getting a master's degree or national certification, acting as a mentor, teaching summer school, or performing other jobs within the school system.

---

**HELP WANTED: EDUCATOR**

Southern university invites applications for two permanent faculty positions in accounting. Applicants at the associate or assistant rank with teaching and research interests in tax and/or accounting information systems are preferred. Doctorate required. Professional certification desirable.

## College Teaching

In postsecondary teaching positions, salaries vary according to faculty rank, type of institution, geographic region, and teaching field. In general, educators at four-year institutions earn more than those who teach at two-year schools and community colleges. According to a survey by the American Association of University Professors, salaries for full-time faculty average $64,455. Professors average $86,437; associate professors, $61,732; assistant professors, $51,545; instructors, $37,737; and lecturers, $43,914. Private independent institutions' salaries are higher than public institutions', but public institutions' salaries exceed salaries in religious-affiliated private institutions. Many faculty members earn additional income through consulting, teaching extra courses, conducting research, or writing for publications.

Benefits are usually less for part-time faculty than for full-time faculty. Special benefits may include tuition waivers for dependents and paid sabbatical leaves.

# Career Outlook

If teaching accounting is your true calling, you can expect to find a good job market over the next several years. This is true whether you plan to teach in a high school or in a college.

### High School Teaching

Over the next decade, job opportunities for secondary school teachers will vary from good to excellent. Most job openings will be attributable to the expected retirement of a large number of teachers and to relatively high turnover rates. Competition for qualified teachers between some localities will

---

**HELP WANTED: EDUCATOR**

Our College of Business Administration is seeking an accounting professor as a full-time faculty member. The applicant must demonstrate strong teaching qualifications and possess a Ph.D. with an emphasis in accounting. In addition to teaching, the successful candidate will assist in the implementation of an M.B.A. degree program and a major in accounting to be launched next year. Application deadline is next month. Send a letter of application, résumé, transcripts, and three letters of reference.

likely continue, with schools luring teachers from other states and districts with bonuses and higher pay. Teachers who are geographically mobile and who obtain licensure in more than one subject should have a distinct advantage in finding a job. The effects of the No Child Left Behind Act remain to be seen, but it may well lead to increased funding for well-qualified teachers.

### College Teaching

Employment of college and university faculty—many of them part-time— is expected to grow much faster than the average for all occupations. This growth is due to the increased enrollments in higher education institutions and retirement of current faculty hired in the 1960s and 1970s to teach baby boomers. Opportunities for teacher applicants holding doctoral degrees are expected to be somewhat better than in previous decades. The number of earned doctorate degrees is projected to rise at a sharply lower rate than over the previous decade, but competition will remain tight for those seeking tenure-track positions at four-year colleges and universities, as many of the job openings are expected to be either part-time or renewable, term appointments.

## Strategy for Finding the Jobs

As with any job search, you need to be aggressive in tracking down your desired teaching job. Here are some useful strategies for seeking teaching positions:

1. Search Internet job banks.
2. Each day, check newspaper ads in the cities in which you would like to work. Many local papers are available online.
3. Review educational statistics and projections to find areas experiencing teacher shortages.
4. Send your résumé and credentials directly to the school districts you are interested in.
5. Attend job fairs. These are sponsored by various states, universities, or associations.

For postsecondary teaching opportunities, you can also consult publications of the various professional accounting societies. There are also special publications about higher education that identify faculty employment opportunities. These resources are available in libraries.

---

**HELP WANTED: EDUCATOR**

Our College of Business is seeking a tenure-track assistant/associate professor of accounting. Teaching responsibilities include graduate courses in financial accounting and undergraduate accounting courses. Required: Ph.D. or D.B.A. in accounting (prefer degree in hand, dissertation defense scheduled soon considered). The position requires demonstrated ability in teaching and potential for service and research/creative activity. CPA or other professional certification and work experience in accounting preferred. The salary is from $55,000. To apply, send letter of application, addressing above qualifications with current vitae (including e-mail address), names, telephone numbers, and e-mail addresses of three professional/academic references. Include a one-page statement of your teaching philosophy, list of preferred teaching assignments, and service and research interests.

---

# Accounting Education in Canada

The Department of Human Resources Development Canada reports the following information on the education requirements and work prospects for secondary school teachers and university professors in Canada.

### High School Teaching

High school teachers must have a bachelor's degree in education, which is usually preceded with specialized training or experience in accounting. Additionally, the secondary school teachers must have teaching certificates from the provinces or territories in which they teach. Nearly one-fourth of new teachers have graduate degrees.

The outlook for high school teachers is fair. This rating is affected by the fact that there were recent government cuts to education, though funding should be increasing soon and creating job openings. Additional job openings will result from an above-average number of retirees in the next several years. Another factor influencing this outlook is the fact that the average hourly wage for secondary school teachers, C$25.93, is above the average for all occupations. New teachers can expect to earn C$16.05 per hour.

### College Teaching

University professors must have doctorate degrees in their areas of specialization. Experience in research, teaching, and leadership is helpful, and improving interpersonal skills and staying current on accounting issues and current events enhance job opportunities. Online education continues to grow, so computer skills continue to be important.

Work prospects for university professors are good. Job openings are resulting from retiring workers and from increased government spending on education and research. Hourly wages, at C$28.77, are above average, but the rate of wage growth is below average.

## Professional Associations

**American Accounting Association**
5717 Bessie Dr.
Sarasota, FL 34233
http://aaahq.org

**American Association of University Professors**
1012 14th St. NW, Suite 500
Washington, DC 20005
aaup.org

**American Federation of Teachers**
555 New Jersey Ave. NW
Washington, DC 20001
aft.org

**The Canadian Academic Accounting
   Association**
3997 Chesswood Dr.
Toronto, ON M3J 2R8
Canada
caaa.ca

**Foundation for Accounting Education**
530 Fifth Ave., 5th Floor
New York, NY 10036

**National Education Association**
1201 16th St. NW
Washington, DC 20036
nea.org

# Interviews with Professionals

The four accounting professionals profiled here each followed a unique career path that led to teaching others how to be accountants.

## Meet John A. Tracy

John A. Tracy earned his undergraduate degree at Creighton University in Omaha, Nebraska, in 1956; his M.B.A. from the University of Wisconsin in 1960; and his Ph.D. from the University of Wisconsin in 1961. A licensed CPA in the state of Colorado, he currently serves as a professor of accounting at the College of Business Administration at the University of Colorado at Boulder. His book, *Accounting for Dummies*, published by IDG Books, is going into its second printing.

"After being a member of the business faculty at the University of California at Berkeley for four years, I joined the faculty at Colorado in 1965, where I have remained since," he says. "Actually it all began when I was tested in my freshman year at Iowa State University. The test results said I should be an accountant, which, to tell the truth, surprised me. So I transferred to Creighton University and majored in accounting. Subsequently, I went to work for Arthur Young and Company (now Ernst & Young), and then went on to graduate school. I have been teaching ever since. Coincidentally, I was recently asked to be retested as part of the update of the same test I took as a freshman. I still test out very high on the accounting scale. That might explain the fact that I have continued to enjoy this field and have never had any second thoughts about the career path I chose.

"Teaching university students for about 36 years has never been dull. From the student riots in my last year at Berkeley through today, the work has provided a never-ending challenge. Students, down deep, are still very much the same. I have not noticed any better or worse preparation in the students of today as compared with students from the 1960s. I would make only one exception—I think that the students today might be a bit more spoiled, not always appreciating how hard their parents had to sacrifice to get to where they are today. I dislike seeing the students who do not work hard and think the world owes them a good living. The best aspect of the job is those students who appreciate the opportunities of a good education and make the most of their college years."

John has come to recognize the importance of being a good listener. Often it is emphasized that accountants need to communicate well orally and in writing, but good communication is spoken *and* heard. John also advises accountants to capitalize on any good fortune and stay current on what's going on elsewhere in the world and in other professions.

## Meet Jay H. Price

Jay H. Price graduated from the University of Wisconsin in Madison with a bachelor of business administration degree (B.B.A.) in accounting. He was employed at Arthur Andersen and Company in Chicago from 1949 until 1988 and retired as a partner. Presently, he serves as an executive professor of accounting at Utah State University in Logan, Utah, and a visiting professor of business at the University of Wisconsin in Madison, Wisconsin.

"I majored in accounting principally because of the results of Veterans Administration–administered interest and aptitude tests," he says. "When I took them (right after World War II), I didn't know anything about the accounting profession (although I did keep books for school, church, and army organizations).

"I entered public accounting rather than private accounting because it appeared to offer greater variety and a greater opportunity to serve a number of clients and companies. I began my career in 1949 when I was hired on the campus of the University of Wisconsin by Arthur Andersen and Company. I believed that Arthur Andersen was more progressive, innovative, client-oriented, and independent in its thinking than were the larger accounting firms at the time.

"As one advances in this field, the daily routine becomes more varied," he says. "In the years immediately prior to retirement, there was no typical day. Each day's activities could involve work with public utility clients, others in the firm, those in professional accounting organizations (such as AICPA), attorneys, engineers, and regulatory commissions. This would include telephone calls, conferences, meetings with clients and others, research on accounting and regulatory questions, oral and written presentations, expert testimony before regulatory commissions, and a host of other activities.

"My favorite part of the job is the variety and intellectual challenge of the work, including the opportunity to work with clients throughout the world. I found that almost all professionals with whom I had contact had high ethical standards. My least favorite part is never having enough time to study all of the material I felt I needed to know.

"My advice to others considering this field is to align yourself with your temperament and personality. For me, it involved becoming an expert in a specialized area (public utility accounting). This was possible because the Chicago office of Arthur Andersen had a large public utility practice. Others may have the temperament or geographic location to become more broad-based and less specialized."

After his long and successful career in accounting, Jay is well positioned to offer good advice to future accountants. He recognizes that accountants must be well versed in computer technology. They must be open to working conditions they may not prefer, such as long hours, travel, and relocation. Accounting professionals need to continue to learn and should consider sharing that knowledge with others via a postretirement teaching career. But even that job will require continuing education.

## Meet Richard O. Davis

Richard O. Davis earned his B.S. in industrial management from Purdue University, West Lafayette, Indiana, in 1971 and earned a Juris Doctor from Fordham Law School in New York in 1975. He also earned an L.L.M. in taxation in 1993 from Georgetown University Law Center in Washington, D.C., and achieved the status of CPA in Washington, D.C., in 1981 and Virginia in 1982. He presently serves as assistant professor of accounting at Susquehanna University.

"When I had nearly completed my L.L.M. in taxation (a necessary credential to teach tax or law at the university level, in the absence of a Ph.D.), I interviewed at Susquehanna University. When it seemed like a good match from both sides, I received an offer and accepted," he says.

"I had always enjoyed teaching, whether giving seminars or conducting training sessions. I started teaching tax and accounting at the university level in the Washington, D.C., area. This experience heightened my interest, and I decided to pursue the possibility of teaching full-time. I particularly enjoy working with young adults in the classroom and helping them make career decisions.

"I was attracted to the independence and flexibility that the profession offers. I had no false hopes that I would work less. In fact, I work just as hard now as I ever did. But I can choose to work when and where I want, subject to certain restrictions, like class schedules.

"I had previously worked for the federal government (IRS), a Big Six CPA firm, a law firm, and a publishing company. I had difficulty balancing work and family priorities at the CPA firm and law firm. At the publishing company, I got tired of writing about what everyone else was doing. So the teaching profession looked like a promising career in which I could still satisfy my desire for an intellectual challenge and a reasonable family life. I enjoy the diversity of life at the university level, and the students help to keep me young.

"In the fall semester, I usually have a Monday-Wednesday-Friday teaching schedule. In the spring semester, I usually have a Tuesday-Thursday schedule. Teaching days are busy, sometimes hectic, but rarely stressful. I teach about twelve hours a week but spend considerable time advising students and preparing for class. I also usually spend a good bit of time on university service, which includes committee meetings, recruiting, faculty meetings, workshops, and so on. I might average about fifty to fifty-five work hours per week. I also do some consulting for a Big Six accounting firm. Occasionally I am asked to testify as an expert witness in tax cases. In the summer, I spend time researching and writing. I also go to several professional conferences and examine my courses and make adjustments.

"I like the flexibility to control my own life. Except for class schedules and office hours, I can plan my day as I wish. I can do much of my work at home. This gives me a tremendous opportunity to be a major part of my children's lives. I have the obligation to do scholarly research and publish, but I have the academic's delight of choosing whatever I want. I do not have a boss looking over my shoulder all the time. I like working with students and having the opportunity to help them grow intellectually and to plan their futures.

"On the downside," Richard says, "I don't feel that professors are properly appreciated or understood by outsiders. We put in many more hours than people think. Accounting professors usually make more money than other professors, but the amount is still not terribly high. Sometimes it is hard to prioritize the demands of the job (teaching, scholarship, university service, professional service, community service). The tenure process is stressful. This is my sixth year (my tenure year), and if I don't get tenure, I will have to begin looking for another job. Also, it is sometimes frustrating when students don't seem interested in their studies."

To teach accounting at the university level, you must have a Ph.D. or, if you want to teach tax law, a law degree and an advanced degree in law. You should also be a CPA and enjoy teaching. An adjunct position in a small educational setting is a good place to start a postsecondary teaching career. Getting published in an academic journal will also help establish you as a good teaching candidate, and the work necessary for this is not unlike the work you'll have to do as a teacher.

## Meet Lela D. "Kitty" Pumphrey

Lela D. Pumphrey earned her bachelor of science–bachelor of business administration (B.S.B.A.) degree from the University of Southern Mississippi, Hattiesburg, Mississippi, in 1968; an M.B.A. from Arkansas State University, Jonesboro, Arkansas, in 1973; and a Ph.D. from the University of Missouri in Columbia, Missouri, in 1984. She has credentials as a CPA, CIVIA, CGFIVI, and CIA and serves as a professor of accounting at Idaho State University in Pocatello, Idaho.

"After approximately ten years of public accounting experience, I enrolled in a Ph.D. program to prepare myself to teach accounting at the collegiate level," she says. "After completion of my Ph.D., I taught at the University of Arkansas at Little Rock. I wanted to live in the intermountain West and moved to that area in 1988 when I was offered a position at Idaho State University.

"I majored in accounting in undergraduate school because I thoroughly enjoyed the subject. I found intellectual stimulation in the practical application of theoretical accounting. After graduation, I entered public accounting because it offered the opportunity to work for a variety of clients and gave me the opportunity to see a number of industries and specializations firsthand. When I entered the Ph.D. program in accounting, I specialized in the area of governmental accounting and auditing for numerous reasons. One reason was that I had many years of audit experience working with small governments and entities that receive federal funding. Another reason, and perhaps more important, was that I believe in the right of the people to know what their governmental officials are doing with the tax dollars entrusted to them. Public management and public policy are reflected in governmental financial statements.

"I had known since I was quite young that teaching was what I wanted to do. However, I was not sure what I wanted to teach. In college I was intellectually attracted to the study of accounting and I thoroughly enjoyed the practice of public accounting. Also, in high school I had considered a career in politics or law. Governmental accounting allows me to be associated with both of those topics.

"As a professor," Lela says, "I have no typical day. I am in the classroom nine hours a week and perform research every day. I spend a few hours each week consulting with governmental entities and answering specific questions about accounting and financial reporting for governmental entities. Students ask questions and governmental accountants call and ask questions—both require research. Sometimes students have difficulty applying the principles taught in the classroom, so I spend many hours trying to help them understand the principles. I enjoy students and I enjoy consulting with practicing accountants. Because I love my career, I work many hours, not because my employer requires them but because of the way I feel. I do quite a bit of professional development training for practicing accountants. This requires many hours in addition to my university responsibilities. I imagine I work fifty to sixty hours a week, by choice.

"My former students who are working for the state controller are currently engaged in preparing the State of Idaho Comprehensive Annual Financial Report," Lela adds. "They call frequently with questions concerning accounting and financial reporting. They seem to be doing a lot of research on theoretical accounting issues. Also, they are interacting a lot with the various state departments as they attempt to identify accounting and financial reporting issues. Their work has included obtaining a state attorney general's opinion on whether a certain quasigovernmental entity is legally part of the state. I am also providing technical assistance to the state legislative auditor, who must audit the financial statements prepared by the state controller.

"I enjoy the challenge of communicating governmental accounting theory and of helping students understand not only governmental accounting but also accounting in general. The challenge is also the downside—sometimes I fail to teach what I wanted to teach. It is frustrating to understand a broad area as well as I do and be unable to communicate the topic to someone else.

"I believe that there are many students who have no intention of entering governmental accounting but end up there for a variety of reasons and then find it rewarding and fulfilling. I would advise anyone who is interested in teaching to first get some experience in the accounting profession and then enter a Ph.D. program to prepare for the research and teaching of their chosen topic. I am so glad that I had several years of public accounting experience. I learned so much in those years."

# Appendix A

## *Program Descriptions*

## The Bachelor and Master of Accounting Degrees from Utah State University School of Accountancy

Utah State University offers an outstanding accounting education for the serious student seeking a successful career in professional accounting, business, or government. The School of Accountancy enjoys a tradition of providing quality education. It is a member of the Federation of Schools of Accountancy and is accredited by the Association to Advance Collegiate Schools of Business International.

### Requirements for a Bachelor of Accounting
*Entry Requirements.* Students applying to the College of Business must have a minimum ACT composite of 24 and a minimum high school grade point average of 3.5. The following courses are prerequisites to business courses:

- Introduction to Economic Institutions, History, and Principles
- Calculus Techniques
- Business Statistics
- General Psychology or Introductory Sociology

*Core Course Work and Areas of Emphasis.* All bachelor's degree candidates must complete the core requirements of the College of Business plus courses for accounting majors. The School of Accountancy also requires all accounting majors to choose an area of emphasis. Students take an additional six to twelve credit hours in their chosen focus areas.

**College of Business Core Classes:**
Survey of Accounting I and II
Corporate Finance
Fundamentals of Marketing
Production/Operations Management
Spreadsheets and Databases for Business
Business Communication
Discussions with Business Leaders
Introduction to Microeconomics
International Economics for Business
Legal and Ethical Environment of Business
Managing Organizations and People
Business Strategy in an Entrepreneurial Context or Business Strategy in
　a Global Context

**Accounting Major Requirements:**
Intermediate Financial Accounting and Reporting I and II
Strategic Cost Management
Income Taxation I
Accounting Information Systems
Auditing Principles and Techniques

**Areas of Emphasis:**
Accounting
Accounting and Economics Dual Major
Business Information Systems
Economics
Finance
Human Resource Management
Management
Marketing
Personal Financial Planning
Production

## Requirements for a Master of Accounting

*Entry Requirements.* Applicants may apply for admission to the program during their last thirty credits of undergraduate study. Accounting and nonaccounting majors are encouraged to apply. Candidates are selected based on the combined consideration of their score on the Graduate Management Admissions Test (GMAT) and their grade point average from their previous ninety quarter hours. Generally, these must total at least 1,150 using the following formula: $(200 \times GPA) + GMAT\ Score \geq 1,150$.

**Core Course Work and Areas of Emphasis.** To receive the master of accounting degree, a student who holds a bachelor's degree in accounting must complete thirty-three credits beyond the requirements for the undergraduate degree. (There is a separate program for master's students with nonaccounting bachelor's degrees.) Students complete a set of core courses in the master's program. They may also choose to pursue an area of emphasis.

**Master of Accounting Core Classes (Other than with Tax Emphasis):**
Income Taxation I and II
Accounting and Reporting for Business Combinations and International
    Issues
Accounting for Government, Nonprofit, and Other Entities and Issues
Financial Auditing
Professional Accounting Cases and Problems
Tax Research and Procedures
Accounting Theory and Research
Business Law and Professional Responsibilities
Communication for Business

**Areas of Emphasis:**
Professional Accountancy
Information Systems
Personal Financial Planning
Finance
Taxation
M.B.A. Accounting

# Appendix B

## Graduate Education

## McIntire School of Commerce at the University of Virginia—Graduate Education

The Master of Science in Accounting–Tax Consulting program at the McIntire School of Commerce enjoys a national reputation. McIntire prepares its degree graduates for the challenges of the dynamic environmental factors that are shaping the accounting profession. The program recognizes that tax professionals are expected to be analysts and problem solvers who bring their specialized knowledge of taxation to bear on an entity's planning and strategy. The degree work also develops the tax consultant's decision-making skills. Program graduates work for corporations, public accounting firms, not-for-profits, and the government. The degree can be completed in one year. Candidates for the program must have a bachelor's degree, official GMAT scores, Test of English as a Foreign Language (TOEFL) scores (for nonnative English speakers), and a minimum grade of B in the prerequisite courses of Introduction to Accounting I and II, Intermediate Accounting, and Federal Taxation I.

### Requirements for Master of Science in Accounting–Tax Consulting

Candidates for the M.S. in Accounting–Tax Consulting program must complete thirty graduate course credits that are offered in a lockstep schedule.

**Required Courses:**
Strategic Business Advising and Communication
Accounting Policy
Business Risk and Business Controls

Research, Analysis, Writing, and Communication
Tax Jurisprudence: Pervasive Tax Doctrines and Their Practical
   Applications
Tax Strategies for Limited Liability Companies and Other Conduit
   Entities
Tax Strategies for Corporations and Shareholders
Corporate Mergers, Acquisitions, Divisions, and Recapitalizations
Tax Strategies for the Executive and the Entrepreneur
International Business and Investment Transactions
Independent Study, Research, and Writing
Overseas Study—International Business, Finance, and Taxation

## Combined Juris Doctor/Master of Science in Accounting Degree Program

Individuals admitted to the School of Law can earn both the J.D. and the M.S. in accounting degrees. Individuals must apply for admission to the McIntire School of Commerce in the usual manner. Commerce studies usually begin after one year in the School of Law. A student may receive up to twelve of the eighty-six credits for the J.D. degree by successfully completing graduate-level course work in the School of Commerce. Similarly, a student may receive up to six of the thirty credits required for the M.S. degree by successfully completing course work in the School of Law.

# Additional Resources

College Board Staff. *The College Board Index of Majors and Graduate Degrees.* New York: College Board, 2004.

Department of Human Resources Development Canada. Job Futures. jobfutures.ca.

Educational Testing Service. The Praxis Series: Professional Assessments for Beginning Teachers. Princeton, NJ: Educational Testing Service, 2004. ets.org.

Farr, Michael. *O\*NET Dictionary of Occupational Titles.* Compiled by Laurence Shatkin. Indianapolis: JIST Works, 2004.

Government of Canada. Canada Site. canada.gc.ca.

———. Jobs, Workers, Training and Careers. jobsetc.ca.

Gulati, Gita, and Nancy R. Binder, eds. *National Directory of Internships.* Boston: Pearson Custom Publishing, 1998.

Krantz, Les. *Jobs Rated Almanac.* Fort Lee, NJ: Barricade Books, 2002.

Macmillan Publishing Company Staff. *Career Information Center.* Old Tappan, NJ: Macmillan Reference USA, 2002.

Maxwell, Bruce. *Guide to America's Federal Jobs.* Indianapolis: JIST Works, 2004.

Morkes, Andrew. *Encyclopedia of Careers and Vocational Guidance.* Chicago: Ferguson Publishing Company, 2003.

National O\*NET Consortium. Occupational Information Network (O\*NET). http://online.onetcenter.org.

Office of the Federal Register. *The United States Government Manual.* Washington, DC: U.S. Government Printing Office, 2003.

Peterson's Guides Staff. *Graduate Programs in Business, Education, Health, Information Studies, Law and Social Work 2004.* Lawrenceville, NJ: Peterson's, 2003.

————. *Peterson's Complete Guide to Colleges.* Lawrenceville, NJ: Peterson's, 2002.

Porter Sargent Staff, eds. *The Handbook of Private Schools.* Boston: Porter Sargent Publishers, Inc., 2004.

Public Service Commission of Canada. Jobs.gc.ca. http://jobs.gc.ca.

Stelzer, Richard J. *How to Write a Winning Personal Statement for Graduate and Professional School.* Lawrenceville, NJ: Peterson's, 1993.

U.S. Department of Labor. Bureau of Labor Statistics. *Occupational Outlook Handbook. 2004–05.* bls.gov/oco. Also available in print. Washington, DC: U.S. Government Printing Office, 2004.

————. *Occupational Outlook Quarterly Online.* Spring 2004. http://stats.bls.gov/opub/ooq/ooqhome.htm. Also available in print. *Occupational Outlook Quarterly.*

U.S. Office of Personnel Management. USAJOBS. usajobs.opm.gov.

VGM Career Books Staff. *VGM's Careers Encyclopedia.* New York: McGraw-Hill Companies, 2001.

# Index